In The Nursery

CREATIVE QUILTS AND DESIGNER TOUCHES

Jennifer Sampou & Carolyn Schmitz

PHOTOGRAPHY BY PHYLLIS BELKIN

C&T PUBLISHING

C&T Publishing
© 2001 Jennifer Sampou and Carolyn Schmitz
Illustrations © C&T Publishing, Inc.

Editor: Candie Frankel
Assistant Editor: Joyce Engels Lytle
Technical Editor: Carolyn Aune
Copy Editor: Steve Cook
Photography: Phyllis Belkin
Design Director, Cover and Book Designer: Christina Jarumay
Illustrator: Rose Sheifer – Graphic Productions
Production Coordinator: Diane Pedersen
Production Assistants: Claudia Boehm, Stephanie Muir, Adia Reid
Cover Image: Room 3: Little Red Hen
Published by C&T Publishing, Inc., P.O. Box 1456, Lafayette, California 94549

Attention Teachers:
C&T Publishing, Inc. encourages you to use this book as a text for teaching. Contact us at
800-284-1114 or www.ctpub.com for more information about the C&T Teachers Program.

Library of Congress Cataloging-in-Publication Data
Sampou, Jennifer
  In the nursery : creative quilts and designer touches / Jennifer
Sampou and Carolyn Schmitz.
          p. cm.
Includes bibliographical references and index.
  ISBN 1-57120-152-1
 1. Quilting–Patterns. 2. Nurseries. 3. Handicraft. 4. Interior
decoration. I. Schmitz, Carolyn II. Title.
  TT835 .S26 2000
  746.46'041–dc21
                                                00-010469

Printed in China
10 9 8 7 6 5 4 3 2 1

Acknowledgments

We could not have created this book without the generous help, support, and knowledge of many people. Thanks to our marvelous husbands, Todd Hensley and Peter Schmitz; Phyllis Belkin for her creativity and beautiful photography; the talented Mabeth Oxenreider, who picked up the pieces and made our designs finished quilts; Candie Frankel for her creative word sense and precise editing; Christina Jarumay and her incredible eye for book design, Joyce Lytle and Carolyn Aune for their technical editing greatness, and the entire C&T Publishing crew; Mom, for last-minute sewing projects and excellent ideas; Carolie Hensley for her valuable input and yards of fabric and for entertaining Thomas; Vivian Camara for her tireless assistance; the Kaufman family and the staff at Robert Kaufman Company for doing such a great job with Jennifer's fabrics; the little angels who modeled—Ariel, Aubrey, Chase, Ella, Lily, Oscar, and Sophie; the fifth grade class at The Pennfield School for sharing their creative writing; Cathy Smith at Goodnight Room; and Alex Anderson, Trish Baizer, Susan Beck, Bonnie Fischer, Anne Glazzard, Wendy Gould, Michele and Jon Henderson, Lyn Lackey, Gloria MacKenzie, Bobbie McIntire, Kathy Messinger, Wendy Neale, Margaret Peters, Merriam Saunders, Kit Seabring, Ana Walker, and Betty Ann Watts. Thank you!

Dedication

To our mother, Elsa Sampou

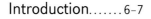

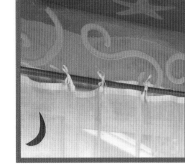

Introduction

The joy of expecting a first baby is a heady emotion for new parents-to-be. The weeks and months before a baby's birth are spent partly in reverie and daydreams about the future and partly, especially as the birth date draws near, in busy and practical preparations. You know that the nesting instinct has kicked in when you start cleaning out the medicine cabinet and chasing down every last cobweb with the vacuum. Preparing and outfitting the nursery is often the final stage before you welcome your little arrival home.

In this book, we'll show you how to put together your own perfect, personal nursery. There are eight different rooms to choose from, each with its own theme, style, color scheme, and mood. Each room's centerpiece is a handmade quilt, which you can sew yourself using the project directions and patterns provided. But you don't have to be a quilter to benefit from the many other craft and design ideas we offer. We focus on easy techniques to help you get a designer look without spending a fortune.

Writing a book on babies' and toddlers' rooms was a natural for us. As professional designers, we're tuned into the world of color, light, and form. Design problems intrigue us, and we love to search for good, workable solutions to the everyday design flaws and challenges we all face in our homes. As sisters, we have the added benefit of our shared childhood memories. The home our parents made for us was comfortable, colorful, warm-hearted, and cheerful. As adults with families of our own, we appreciate more than ever the value of creating a loving atmosphere where we and our families can thrive.

If you're thinking, "I don't know where to start," then let us give you a hand. Together, we'll explore how color can make a room soft and restful, or rev things up. You'll learn our secret thoughts about accessories and how we go about choosing them—often picking from stuff we already own—to play up a room's theme and ambiance. And don't expect us to be conventional when it comes to furniture—we'll show you options you may not have even thought of for storing baby's clothing and paraphernalia. We can't promise to tell you everything, but when you're ready to learn more about decorative painting or need help brushing up on your quilting and sewing skills, our source guide will point you in the right direction.

We hope the ideas and projects in the pages that follow will inspire your nursery's decor and help you get your project off the ground. Whether you're newly pregnant or ready to give your toddler's room an overhaul, creating a new decor can be an overwhelming task. We're here to make it affordable and fun.

A Sweet Lullaby

On balmy summer nights, Victorian families made use of screened-in sleeping porches. Beds or cots were moved out onto the porch, where sleepy children could catch a cool evening breeze and escape the stuffy heat indoors. To turn this sleeping porch into a seasonal nursery, we add familiar and readily available Victorian era touches, such as white wicker, potted plants, and vintage linens and toys. The family tree floorcloth is sure to become a future heirloom. The simple two-tone silhouette is easy to paint on canvas, and the soothing colors enhance the standard gray porch floor. Visiting relatives will enjoy locating their names among the branches as they trace baby's lineage.

A porch bedroom encourages nothing more strenuous than sitting in a rocker, cooing and singing lullabies to baby, and cooling off on a hot summer's day. Perhaps grandmother will create this airy retreat at her house for the days when baby comes to visit.

> "Where did you come from baby dear? Out of the every-where into here."

— GEORGE MACDONALD

Designer
Touches

Antique doorknobs substitute for hooks on a wall-mounted rack.

Wall and floor paints from Benjamin Moore; see Sources.

An organza canopy cascades gently around the head of the bassinet. Sewn to a wire hoop and suspended from the ceiling, this inexpensive addition diffuses the sunlight. Note how the ethereal volume makes baby's bed the focal point.

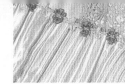

Hush Little Baby

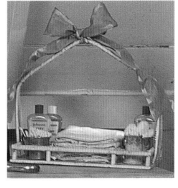

Collections of antique dolls or infants' clothing make sweet displays. If you saved your childhood doll collection or have old handmade baby clothes stashed in the attic, the cost can be nil.

Old wicker furniture is easily revived with spray paint. Check out the new colors at your local hardware store, and follow the manufacturer's instructions for safe use.

A quilt rack displays baby blankets, quilts, and precious linens. An old-fashioned wooden drying rack would also work.

Silver baby cups serve as holders for cotton balls and swabs. Store the cups in a wicker caddy for easy toting to the changing table.

Designed and made by Carolyn Schmitz with inspiration from Judith Baker Montano; 29" x 41".

Victorian Crazy Quilt

Baby's crazy quilt is done in a white and ivory palette instead of the traditional kaleidoscope of colors. In addition to new cuttings of silk and satin, the "fabrics" include scraps of lace from Carolyn's wedding dress and pillowcase trims crocheted by her grandmother. You can add sentimental value by sewing in your family-owned laces and linens, but don't forget that you can also purchase vintage pieces. Old linens don't have to be perfect. With a crazy quilt approach, you can recycle the good parts of textiles that are partly damaged.

Supplies

Muslin: 1 yard, washed and pressed

White and ivory fabrics: 1 1/2 to 2 yards assorted satins, brocades, crepes, and taffetas. You might include scraps from Grandma's sewing basket, used linens and clothing, or finds from a bridal fabric shop or antique store.

White or ivory cotton sateen: 1/2 yard for border

Trims: 6 to 7 yards assorted laces (e.g., Battenburg, Cluny, Irish) and shirred ribbons. Individual lace motifs may also be used. Pieces may be new, old, or used.

Hangers: 3/4 yard of 7/8"-wide ribbon.

Border trim: 4 yards 1"-wide lace

Backing: 1 1/2 yards neutral fabric

Batting, lightweight (such as Thermore®): 29 1/2" x 41 1/2"

Cutting

Muslin:
   Cut four 13 1/2" x 20" rectangles for the foundation.
Cotton sateen:
   Cut five 2 1/2"-wide strips. Piece as necessary to cut two 34 1/2" strips and two 47 1/2" strips for the border.
Backing:
Cut one 29 1/2" x 41 1/2" rectangle.

Block Assembly

1. To make the crazy quilt patches, cut the white and ivory fabric assortment into approximately 40 randomly sized strips, 3" to 4" wide and 6" to 10" long.

2. Select a 4" x 5" strip for patch 1 (the center patch). Trim the strip so it has 5 or 6 sides of different lengths.

3. Lay one muslin rectangle flat. Place patch 1 on it, right side up and centered. Select a strip for patch 2. Place it on patch 1, right sides together and with one edge aligned. Machine-stitch 1/4" from the aligned edges through all layers. Flip the top patch over and press.

4. Cut a length of lace or ribbon trim to cover the seam just sewn. Stitch the trim in place, concealing the seam.

5. Select a strip for patch 3. Place it face down on patches 1 and 2. Machine-stitch along one edge of patch 3 through all layers, making a 1/4" seam. Trim away any excess bulk along the seam, then flip the top patch over and press. Conceal this seam with a new trim, as in step 4.

6. Repeat step 5, adding patches and trims one by one, until the entire foundation is covered. Try overlapping the fabrics and trims to form triangles and other interesting shapes. You can plan your arrangement in advance or develop it as you go along. In some areas of the block, you may wish to sew several patches together and then stitch them to the foundation as a unit. You might also try omitting the lace or ribbon trim from some seams.

7. Repeat steps 2–6 to make four crazy quilt blocks total. The blocks do not need to be identical in layout. Trim each block to 13" x 19".

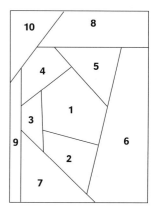

Quilt Assembly

1. Sew the blocks together in a Four-Patch, making $1/4"$ seams. Press seams open.

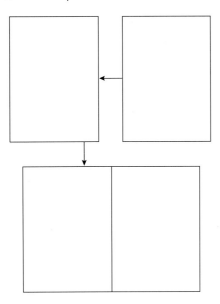

2. Sew the border strips to the top, bottom, and sides with $1/4"$ seams, starting and stopping $1/4"$ from each corner of the Four-Patch panel. Press the seam allowance toward the border after each application. Miter the corners (refer to a basic quiltmaking book for more details).

3. Pin the 1"-wide lace trim to the border, mitering the corners. Topstitch in place. Pin and topstitch an embroidered hem from a bed sheet across the top and an embroidered family initial from a dinner napkin in the middle (see photos on page 14 and at right).

4. To make ribbon hangers shown on page 12, cut three 8" pieces of ribbon. Fold each piece in half and baste to the top edge of the quilt, raw edges even; place one ribbon at the middle and the other two 4" from each side. The hangers will be permanently attached when the backing and top are stitched together.

5. Lay the backing and top right sides together, then lay the batting on top. Pin. Stitch $1/4"$ from the edge all around, leaving an opening for turning at the bottom. Clip the corners, trim the batting close to the stitching, and turn right side out. Stitch the opening by hand.

6. To quilt the wall hanging, stitch-in-the-ditch along the vertical, horizontal, and border seams. Hand-embroider a few decorative stitches such as French knots to stabilize the quilt.

7. Add buttons and charms to finish only if the quilt will be used as a wall hanging. On a baby's crib quilt, they pose a choking hazard.

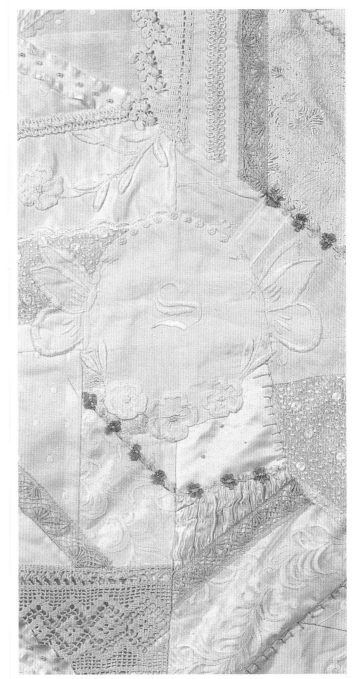

Keepsake Box

Designed and made by Wendy Neale; 9" x 9" x 4". Use this box to collect and store family mementos for the next generation.

Supplies

9" x 9" x 4" box with lid (we used a papier-mâché box from a craft store)

Fabric for box: 3/4 yard

Contrasting fabric for lining: 3/4 yard

Thin quilt batting: 9" square for lid, 6 1/2" square for picture frame

1/16"-thick cardboard: 6 1/2" square for picture frame

Posterboard: 22" x 28"

White glue and/or spray adhesive

Small brush for applying glue

Sharp scissors

Craft knife

Straight-edge ruler

Cover the Box and Lid

1. Cut a piece of fabric to fit around the box plus 3/4" and to extend 5/8" beyond the top and bottom edges.

2. Brush a thin layer of white glue on one side of the box. Position the fabric on it, beginning with a 3/8" overlap at the corner edge, and smooth in place. Repeat to glue fabric to each side of the box. When you reach the starting point, fold in the raw edge and glue securely. If the fabric is thick or bulky, trim off the flap and glue it flat.

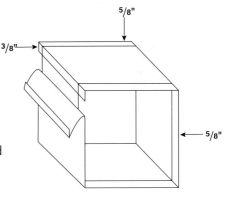

3. Turn the box so the base faces up. Pinch the fabric at each corner and cut off the excess. Glue down the flaps.

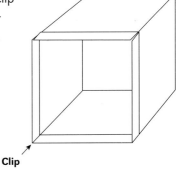

4. At the open end, clip fabric at each corner and glue the flaps to the inside.

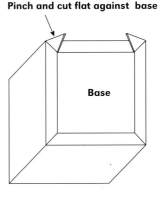

5. Glue the 9" square of batting to the lid top.

6. Cut a piece of fabric to cover the top and sides of the box lid plus 1/2" all around. Lay the fabric square wrong side up on a flat surface. Brush glue on two opposite side edges of the lid, then center the lid, batting side down, on the fabric. Fold the fabric up onto the glued edges so it stretches evenly over the batting; hold in place until glue sets.

7. Turn the lid right side up. At each corner, pinch and crease the fabric, and trim off the excess flap to 1/2".

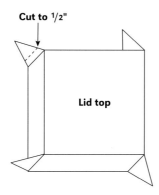

Cut to 1/2"

Lid top

8. Turn the lid over, so the inside faces up. At each corner, open the flap, reverse the fold, and glue one layer against the side of the lid. Brush glue along the inside edges of the two sides you have already glued. Fold the fabric to the inside and press in place.

9. Brush glue onto the remaining two outside edges. Press the fabric in place, tucking in the excess at each corner. Clip if necessary to reduce bulk.

10. Fold and glue the remaining fabric to the inside.

Line the Box and Lid

1. Measure one inside wall of the box. From posterboard, cut four rectangles this size. Trim off a scant 1/8" from the length and width of each rectangle. From lining fabric, cut four rectangles 3/8" larger all around.

2. Lay one lining rectangle wrong side up. Brush a light coat of glue on a posterboard rectangle and press it, glue side down, on the fabric. Smooth the fabric from the right side. Trim the corners as shown. Fold over and glue down the top flap only. Repeat for all four pieces.

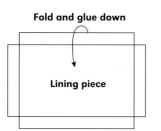

Fold and glue down

Lining piece

3. Apply glue to one inside wall of the box. Extend the glue onto the box floor and adjacent side walls for 3/8".

4. Position a posterboard piece on this wall, fabric side out, so the top edge falls a scant 1/8" below the box rim. Press firmly to adhere the piece and its three loose flaps.

5. Working clockwise, brush glue on the next inside wall, including the floor and adjacent wall to the right. Fold over

and glue down the left flap of the second posterboard piece. Glue this piece in place, concealing the right flap of the first piece. Repeat this step once more to line the third wall. Fold over and glue both side flaps of the fourth piece before gluing it in place.

6. Repeat steps 1 and 2 to cut and line a posterboard piece for the box floor. Fold over and glue down all the flaps, then glue in place. Line the box lid in the same way.

Photo Frame

1. Cut a 6 1/2" square from posterboard. Trim off a scant 1/8" from the length and width. Cut a piece of lining fabric to this size, but add 5/8" to the bottom edge. Glue the fabric to the posterboard. Fold over and glue down the 5/8" flap. Set this piece aside.

2. Using a ruler and pencil, draw a 4 1/2" square, centered, on the 6 1/2" cardboard square. Cut out the inner square for the picture opening. To pad the frame, cut and glue on a matching piece of batting.

3. Cut a piece of the box fabric 5/8" larger than the frame all around. Lay the fabric wrong side up, and center the frame, batting side down, on top. Fold and glue the bottom flap onto the frame back.

4. Carefully cut the fabric inside the picture opening to within 5/8" of the inner edge. Clip diagonally into the corners.

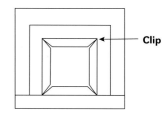

Clip

5. Fold the four inner flaps onto the frame back and glue down.

6. Pinch the fabric at the two top corners and cut off the excess to reduce bulk. Place the backing piece from step 1 on the frame back, wrong side up and bottom edges aligned. Fold the remaining three flaps onto the backing and glue them down. Slide your baby's photograph into the frame through the bottom opening.

7. Glue the frame to box lid. Add lace or ribbons if desired.

Family Tree Floorcloth

Designed and made by Carolyn Schmitz for her children, Dylan and Chlöe, whose names appear on the trunk; 36" x 60". See Sources to order canvas.

Supplies

Floorcloth canvas, preprimed, cut to 38" x 62"

Acrylic craft paints in 2-oz. containers:

    4 peach

    1 blue-gray

    1 pale green

    1 dark green

    1 white

Black fine-point permanent marker

Acrylic varnish

White craft or fabric glue

Assorted artist brushes

Plate for palette

Ruler and pencil

Scissors

Tracing paper on roll

Transfer paper or chalk

Heavy books

List of relatives' birthdays and wedding dates

Assembly

1. Lay canvas right side up on a flat surface. Draft a line 1" in from the edge all around. Trim off the corners diagonally. Turn the canvas over. Fold in all four edges on the marked lines, mitering the corners. Glue in place (be generous with glue). Weight edge with heavy books, and let dry overnight.

2. Using a wide brush, paint the right side of the canvas peach. Brush right up to and onto the folded edge. Let dry 30 minutes. Paint additional coats as needed for full coverage.

3. Draft a 3 1/2"-wide border on the canvas all around. Paint the border pale green. Let dry. Paint a narrow dark green stripe along the inner border to outline and set off the peach interior.

4. Sketch a tree on a 28" x 52" piece of tracing paper (see the sample sketch on page 90). Add limbs and branches as needed to accommodate the family members on your list. Transfer the sketch onto the floorcloth, or copy it freehand with chalk.

5. On a plate or palette, mix blue-gray and white paint to create light, medium, and dark values. Paint the tree trunk, branches, and leaves, using the lighter value in the interior areas and the medium and darker values toward the edges. Let dry overnight.

6. Write your family names and dates on the tree using a black fine-point permanent pen.

7. Apply three coats of acrylic varnish and let dry, following the manufacturer's directions.

Run Bunny Run

Blue and white is one of those appealing color combinations that works equally well for a baby boy or girl. In this north-facing room, the periwinkle blue walls are forever changing in the soft light. To enhance the heavenly atmosphere, we applied the same hue at half-strength to the ceiling. White woodwork sets off the grand architecture, while the honey-toned floor adds the perfect color wheel complement.

The room's blue and white quilted wall hanging prompted our search for additional bunny-themed accessories. An old iron bunny and a porcelain bunny were among our finds, and a young artist volunteered an original bunny painting. More animals appear on the découpage wastebasket and a set of antique stacking blocks, adding their own touch of whimsy as well as some brighter color notes. In the center of the room, an oval rug from Judi Boisson draws all eyes to the crib. As you gaze down at baby, you're bound to smile at the white pompom "cottontails" edging the bedding.

Designer
Touches

✳ Ceilings don't have to be white. Coloring or tinting a ceiling can enhance the ambiance of a room tremendously. For a basic tint, ask the paint store to mix a quarter- to half-strength recipe of your wall color in a flat finish.

Bunnies run across the grass.
Sometimes I don't even know they've passed.
—BEN FERNANDEZ, AGE 10

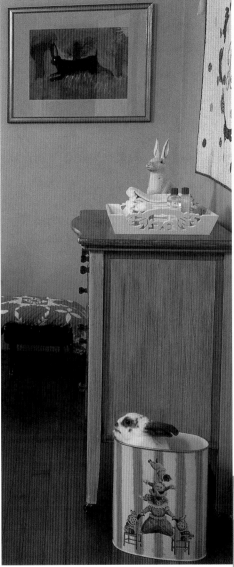

✳ "Float" the crib so you can approach it from either side. Instead of placing a crib flush against the wall, stand it on a rug "island" in the middle of the room. This layout looks best in large rooms with high ceilings.

✳ Recycle old bedspreads to make valances and dust ruffles. Bedspreads yield ample fabric for large projects, and if you shop at thrift and rummage sales, the cost can be quite reasonable. Work the existing bedspread fringe into your design to avoid further hemming.

Wall and ceiling paints from Benjamin Moore; see Sources.

✳ Hang children's artwork on the walls. For a professional look, slip that crayon drawing or tempera painting into a frame. An older sibling or cousin might like to contribute a special piece of art for the new baby's room.

✳ Shade pulls are always hard to reach on tall windows. Instead of a traditional cord and ring, use a length of tulle weighted with a handmade glass star, a sturdy Christmas ornament, or a small toy. If the pull will show in your window, it's worth using something special.

Designed by the authors using Jennifer Sampou fabrics
(see Sources for details); assembled by Mabeth Oxenreider; 36" x 50".

Run Bunny Run Quilt

Memories of our childhood pets inspired the bunny motif for this simple, elegant wall hanging. The ten bunnies hop in an oval around the word "Baby," but you could easily substitute your little one's first name. All the appliqués are cut from assorted blue fabrics, fused in place, and machine-satin-stitched. Randomly spaced polka dots lend a carefree, playful touch, and blue binding provides a classic finish.

Supplies

White-on-white check: 1 1/2 yards for background
Blue to periwinkle prints: 8 to 10 assorted 5" x 7" scraps for bunnies and dots; one fat quarter for name; 3/8 yard for binding
Backing: 1 1/2 yards
Batting, cotton: 40" x 54"
Fusible web: 1 yard

Cutting

White-on-white check:
   Cut one 36" x 50" rectangle.
Blue print:
   Cut five 2"-wide strips; piece end to end for binding.

Assembly

1. Make a bunny template (page 91).

2. Trace the "Baby" pattern (pages 91 and 92). To substitute a name, spell out the name using a computer font, enlarge to approximately 8 1/2" x 11 1/4", and trace the mirror image, using a window or a light box..

3. Using the template and tracing, mark 10 bunnies and 1 "Baby" or name appliqué on the paper backing of fusible web. Also draw 40 freeform circles 1 1/2" across (the size of a large spool of thread). Following the manufacturer's instructions, fuse the web to the appropriate color fabrics and cut out.

4. Lay the background right side up on a flat surface. Center the name appliqué on top. Arrange the bunnies around the appliqué in a 17" x 22" oval (inside measurement). Scatter the dots over the surface, placing some inside the oval. Fuse in place.

5. Stitch around each motif, using a narrow zigzag and matching color thread. Take your time to ensure smooth, even stitching.

6. Layer the top, batting, and backing. Baste with safety pins.

7. Outline-quilt each motif. Stitch a meandering design in the background. Bind to finish.

Bunny Face Pillow

Designed and made by Jennifer Sampou; 14" x 14".

Supplies

Chenille: 1/2 yard each blue and white
Flannel: 6 1/2" square for bunny body
Blue silk ribbon, 4mm-wide: 1 1/2 to 2 yards
Chenille needle, size 18–24
White 1" pompom trim: 1 3/4 yards
Pillow form, 14" square
Water-soluble marker

Cutting

Make templates for body and head (pages 92 and 93).
Blue chenille:

Cut one 15" square and two 5 1/2" x 15" rectangles.

White chenille:

Cut one 7" x 15" rectangle and one head.

Flannel:

Cut one body.

Assembly

1. Lay the blue chenille square right side up. Position the bunny body on top, right side up, and pin. Stitch the edges with a narrow zigzag.

2. Add the bunny head and zigzag as in step 1.

3. Using a water-soluble marker, transfer the bunny face to the head. Embroider the face details with silk ribbon, using satin stitch for nose and eyes and stem stitch for eyebrows and mouth.

4. Pin the pompom trim around the blue chenille square, edges matching and pompoms facing in. Clip to ease the corners. Baste.

5. To make the pillow back, sew the two blue chenille rectangles to the white chenille rectangle along the long edges, using 1/2" seams. Press seam allowances open.

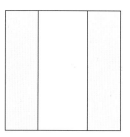

6. Pin the pillow top and back right sides together. Stitch 1/2" from edge all around, leaving an opening for turning. Be careful not to catch pompoms in seam.

7. Trim the corners and turn right side out. Insert the pillow form. Hand-sew the opening.

Warning: Remove pillow when baby is in the crib as the pompoms pose a choking hazard.

Cottontail Bumper Pad

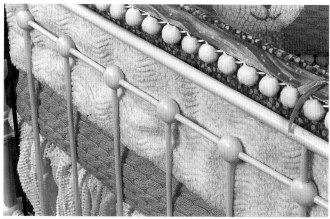

Designed and made by Jennifer Sampou, using Jennifer Sampou fabrics; see Sources for details.

Supplies

Medium blue print: 1 3/4 yards for inside bumper, 1/3 yard for outside bumper top strip
Dark blue print: 1/2 yard for outside bumper middle strip
White chenille: 1 1/4 yards for outside bumper bottom strip
Batting, 10-ounce, 48"-wide: 1 5/8 yards
White 1" pompom trim: 4 1/2 yards
Blue ribbon: 3 1/4 yards for ties.

Cutting

Medium blue print:

Cut five 12"-wide strips. Piece as necessary to cut two 28" lengths and two 53" lengths for inside bumper.
Cut five 2"-wide strips. Piece and cut as above for top outside bumper.

Dark blue print:

Cut five 3"-wide strips. Piece and cut as above for middle outside bumper.

White chenille:

Cut five 9"-wide strips. Piece and cut as above for bottom outside bumper.

Batting: Cut two 12" x 53" pieces and two 12" x 28" pieces.

Assembly

1. Lay one dark blue print strip right side up. Baste pompom trim to one long edge, clipping off excess. Place medium blue strip on top, right sides together, and stitch, catching pompom tape in the $1/2$" seam. Press seam toward dark blue strip. Repeat to make four blue pompom units. Join the dark blue edge of each unit to a white chenille strip using $1/2$" seam. Press toward dark blue.

2. Proceed with the Basic Bumper Pad instructions on page 88. The medium blue print is fabric #1 and the chenille/pompom units are fabric #2. Omit steps 5 and 6.

No-Sew Lampshade Slipcover

Designed and made by Gloria MacKenzie using Jennifer Sampou fabrics; see Sources for details; 8" x 8" x 13" lampshade.

Supplies

Lampshade, white or light-colored
Fabric: $2/3$ yard
Coordinating fabric: $2/3$ yard
Interfacing, stiff fusible: $2/3$ yard
Velcro dots: 3
Kraft paper for pattern
Assorted buttons: 19 to 22
Scissors
Pencil
Hot-glue gun or fabric glue
Fusible tape, $1/2$" wide

Assembly

1. Lay the kraft paper flat. Place the lampshade on the kraft paper, seam side down, about 1" from the edge.

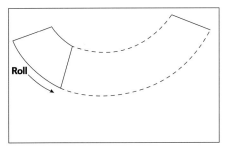

Slowly roll the shade along the paper, marking the top and and bottom edges with a pencil, until the shade has made one complete revolution. You may want to do a dry run first to make sure you won't roll off the paper. Your finished drawing will consist of two large arcs.

2. Cut out the kraft paper pattern, adding a 1" overlap at one end. Test-fit the pattern on the shade. Mark the top and bottom edge even with the shade, and trim as needed. Draft the final pattern, cutting a straight edge for the seam overlap.

3. Use the pattern to cut one fabric and one interfacing for the lampshade slipcover. Fuse the interfacing to the wrong side of the fabric.

4. For a seam band, cut a strip of coordinating fabric 4" wide x the shade width + 1". Turn edges under $1/2$" on both long edges. Fold in half lengthwise. Fuse in place over one end of slipcover. Apply three Velcro dots along band on wrong side, matching other half of dots on other end. Secure with glue.

5. From coordinating fabric, cut two 2"-wide bias strips to fit around the top and bottom rims of shade. Fold strips in half lengthwise and press. Fold each edge to center, and press. Place bias trim over top and bottom edges of shade. Fold under the ends and fuse in place.

6. For button "tufts," cut a 2" x 6" piece of coordinating fabric into 19 to 22 strips each $1/4$" x 2" long. Fold strip over eye of sewing needle, add drop of glue, and poke into holes of buttons from the right side. Glue buttons randomly onto shade cover.

7. Place slipcover over shade, matching the Velcro dots to secure.

Little Red Hen

Step into this combination nursery and play-room and you can almost hear the chickens clucking. All children love picture books about farm animals and learn at a young age how to baa like a sheep, oink like a pig, and quack like a duck. For adults, this nursery is pure nostalgia. It embodies the vintage green, yellow, and red color palette of the 1930s and calls to mind earlier generations when people's everyday chores including milking cows and picking tomatoes ripe from the vine.

Choosing a popular theme for your nursery is a smart move, particularly if your shopping time is lim-ited. You'll be able to draw from a plentiful variety of new and old furnishings; even vintage, one-of-a-kind items tend to be marketed according to popular trends. To develop our farmhouse look, we used wicker, braided rugs, and a wooden country table. An old barn ladder, bolted to the wall, makes an instant display for stuffed toys.

Designer
Touches

Rummage through your family attic to unearth old furniture and decorative items. The toys, wicker couch, and Little Red Hen record all came from Mom's attic. We gave the couch a fresh coat of spray paint and a new cushion. Secondhand furnishings are essential for a vintage look; just make sure old baby items meet current safety standards (see page 110).

Background paints from Benjamin Moore; see Sources. Decorative mural painting by Carolyn Schmitz.

🌸 A painted mural creates a cottage garden right inside the playroom. Add actual objects, such as a folding café chair or a rustic birdhouse, to make the scene appear more three-dimensional. Complex scenes are best painted by a professional artist.

🌸 Use a container collection you already own to hold baby's changing table necessities. Cotton balls and swabs tuck nicely inside glass chicken dishes, giving you the chance to enjoy your collection every day. Just be sure to place breakables at a safe height and not to overdo the "no touch" items.

"Who will plant the wheat?..."

Vintage quilt redesigned by the authors; pieced, appliquéd, and quilted by Mabeth Oxenreider; 44" x 54".

Little Red Hen Quilt

The room's Little Red Hen quilt, with its hand-stitched excerpt, isn't bashful about proclaiming the moral of the familiar farmyard tale. The busy heroine appears four times, practically popping off the quilt at each corner, while her barnyard companions observe quietly from the sidelines. The strong revival of 1930s fabric reproductions in the quilting industry makes it possible to obtain authentic-looking colors and patterns for a quilt of this genre. The graceful scalloped edging is another signature 1930s touch.

Supplies

Yellow-and-white check: 5/8 yard for center panel (use a very low-contrast check to set off the dark green embroidery; cream tone-on-tone or a pale yellow print will also work)

Yellow print: 3/8 yard for accent borders and appliqués

Off-white solid: 3 1/3 yards total: 1 2/3 yards for inner and outer borders, 1 2/3 yards for backing

Green print: 7/8 yard total: 1/4 yard for inner border, 5/8 yard for binding

Red, blue, orange, and green 1930s prints: sixteen 6" squares for appliqués

Pearl cotton #8 in dark green and colors to match barnyard animals

Embroidery needle

Batting: 48" x 58"

Water-soluble marker

Cutting

Yellow-and-white check:

Cut one 17 1/2" x 23 1/2" rectangle for center panel.

Yellow print:

Cut eight 1"-wide strips. Cut into two 23 1/2" lengths, two 18 1/2" lengths, two 40 1/2" lengths, and two 31 1/2" lengths.

Off-white solid:

Cut two 8 1/2" x 30 1/2" strips.

Cut two 6 1/2" x 24 1/2" strips.

Cut four 5 1/2" x 44" strips.

Green print:

Cut two 1 3/4" x 41 1/2" strips.

Cut two 1 3/4" x 34" strips.

Cut a continuous bias strip 2 1/2" wide x 220" long (refer to a basic sewing or quiltmaking book for details).

Appliqué

1. Divide and mark each 8 1/2" x 30 1/2" off-white strip into five 6" sections, allowing an extra 1/4" at each end.

2. Divide and mark each 6 1/2" x 24 1/2" off-white strip into three 8" sections, allowing an extra 1/4" at each end.

3. Lay out these four strips as they will appear in the quilt inner border.

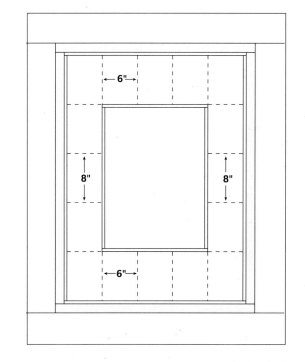

4. Prepare the 16 fusible hen, kitten, piglet, duck, and wheat stalk appliqués (pages 94–97), using the 1930s prints and following the fusible web manufacturer's instructions.

5. Fuse the appliqués to the white inner border strips, referring to the quilt photo, opposite, for placement. Machine-satin-stitch around each motif with matching thread. Hand-embroider the details in stem stitch and satin stitch using pearl cotton.

Quilt Top Assembly

1. Sew the 23 1/2" yellow print strips to side edges of center panel. Press the seams toward the border. Sew the 18 1/2" yellow print strips to the top and bottom edges; press toward the border.

2. Add the white appliquéd inner borders, sides first, then top and bottom; press each seam toward the border as you go.

3. Repeat Step 2 to add the yellow accent border, the green border, and the white outer border.

4. Measure 5" out from the green border and mark a line on the white border all around for the outer edge of the scallop.

5. Make scallop templates A, B, and C (pages 93 and 94). Use template A to mark eight scallops and parallel quilting lines on each side border, beginning and ending 1 1/2" in from the green border corner. In the same way, use template B to mark six scallops on the top and bottom borders. Mark the corners last, using template C.

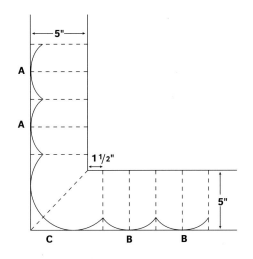

6. Enlarge the nursery rhyme (page 98) 225%. Using a water-soluble marker, trace the nursery rhyme on the center panel.

Quilting and Finishing

1. Layer the quilt top, batting, and backing. Baste with large safety pins.

2. Stitch-in-the-ditch along the three inner borders. Machine-outline each motif.

3. Using dark green pearl cotton, hand-quilt the off-white inner and outer borders on the straight marked lines (do not quilt the scallop curves). Hand-quilt the nursery rhyme using a short running stitch.

4. Fold the green print bias binding strip in half lengthwise. Align raw edges on the marked scallop line, pin, and stitch in place 3/8" from raw edge of the binding. Cut away excess fabric and batting. Fold binding to quilt back and hand-sew to finish.

Two-Tier Dust Ruffle

Designed by Carolyn Schmitz using 1930s reproduction fabrics; made by Elsa Sampou.

Follow the Basic Dust Ruffle instructions on page 89, but gather and sew two tiers to the muslin base instead of one. The top tier is approximately one-half the width of the lower tier.

...asked the Little Red Hen.

"Not I," said the pig, duck,

and cat. So the Little Red

Hen did it herself.

"Who will eat the bread?"

"We will!" the lazy ones

cried. "No," said the Hen,

"I shall eat it."

eilings are not usually focal points, but this room breaks the rules: you can't help but look up at the stunning night sky and fanciful tangerine-colored border. The bright yellow stars, dancing turquoise scrolls, and marching lime dots are sure to make any infant gurgle with pleasure. Baby can gaze up at the stars at every naptime, and you'll get a turn whenever the two of you play "airplane" on the floor. To create this overhead canopy, we painted a larger, bolder version of the bumper pad fabric, an idea you can adapt with other fabric designs to extend a colorful motif around the room.

Once we established the room's stargazing theme, furnishing the room became easy. Novelty star-shaped knobs were a must for a painted chest of drawers, and we couldn't resist padded fabric stars at the ends of the bumper ties. The star wall hanging, a design from Alex Anderson's book *Simply Stars*, uses Jennifer's fabrics in exciting, intense combinations. Softer versions of the same colors turn up in a painted chest, tabletop clock, and wall paints. We kept the same palette for the duvet cover, but switched from stars to soft, bubbly circles to inspire a quieter, more restful mood in the crib.

Designer Touches

Revive old furniture instead of buying new. This chest of drawers used to be ugly: dark brown with clunky metal pulls. Save money by painting it two tones and replacing the dated hardware with festive star-shaped knobs. The result is darling!

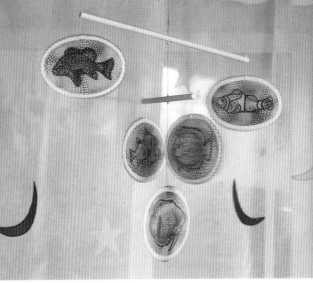

Twinkle

⭐ Area rugs can pick up a room's key colors and motifs. Place small rugs on carpeting or wood floors for an inexpensive mood change.

⭐ Solid-color appliqués give sheer curtains a custom look. Shop for ready-made designs like these star and moon panels, or sew your own.

⭐ Quilts don't have to be in the crib. Their warmth, comfort, and tactile pleasure also make them great wall hangings.

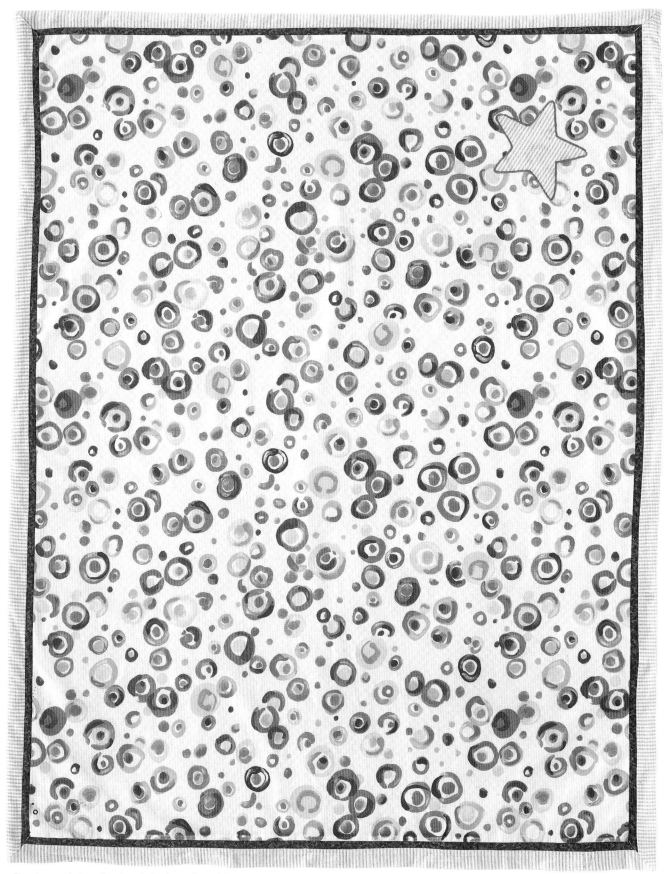

Duvet cover designed and made by the authors; 35" x 49".

Star Bright Crib Duvet Cover

A bubbly print in a cheerful palette of colors makes the perfect duvet cover. The diminutive crib size sews up quick and easy, from the mitered corner borders to the single star appliqué. A baby down comforter purchased from Pottery Barn Kids fits inside. Ribbon ties stitched to the interior seams keep the comforter in place, and lightweight plastic snaps are used for closure at the bottom.

Supplies

Bright print: 1 3/8 yards for center panel
Dark blue: 1/4 yard for inner border
Blue-and-white stripe: 1/2 yard for outer border
Backing: 1 1/2 yards
Ribbon, 5/8" wide: 1 yard for inside ties
Snap Tape™ by Dritz containing 10 snaps
Plastic rings: 4
Fusible web: 6" square

Cutting

Bright print:
  Cut one 32 1/2" x 46 1/2" rectangle for center panel.
Dark blue:
  Cut five 1"-wide strips. Piece as necessary to cut two 41" lengths and two 55" lengths for inner border.
Blue-and-white stripe:
  Cut four 1 3/4"-wide strips. Piece as necessary to cut one 41" length for top outer border and two 55" lengths for side outer borders.
  Cut two 2 5/8"-wide strips. Piece as necessary to cut one 41" length for bottom outer border.
Prepare one star appliqué (page 104), following the fusible web manufacturer's instructions.
Backing:
  Cut one 36" x 52 1/2" rectangle.
Ribbon:
  Cut four 8" pieces.
Snap tape:
  Cut into 5 equal segments containing 2 snaps each.

Assembly

All seams are 1/4" unless otherwise indicated. Zigzag or serge all raw edges to prevent fraying.

1. Sew each dark blue inner border strip to a blue-and-white stripe outer border strip along one long edge. Press the seam toward the blue-and-white strip.

2. Lay the center panel flat, right side up. Place the blue edge of the bottom (wider) border strip along one 32 1/2" edge, right sides together, so the strip overhangs the panel about 4" at each end; pin. Stitch together, starting and stopping 1/4" from each corner of the center panel. Press the seam toward center panel.

3. Fold and press the remaining long edge of the bottom border 1/4" to the wrong side. Fold up again, just beyond the nearest stitching line. Hem by hand, or stitch-in-the-ditch from the right side.

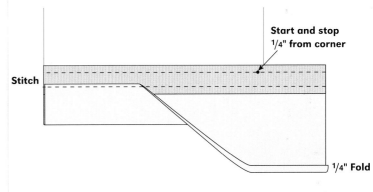

Start and stop 1/4" from corner
Stitch
1/4" Fold

4. Repeat step 2 to join the side and top border strips to the center panel.

5. Lay the panel right side up. At the top right corner, overlap the border strips.

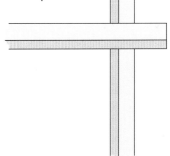

Fold the top border at a 45° angle so the edges and seam lines meet. Topstitch along the mitered fold.

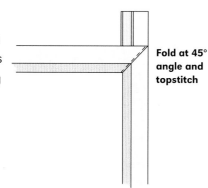

Fold at 45° angle and topstitch

On the underside, cut off the excess fabric 1/4" from stitching. Repeat to miter the top left corner. To miter the bottom corners, start with the side border on top. Fold the miter, topstitch, and trim as before. Press the excess side border to the wrong side, even with the folded bottom edge.

6. Fuse the star to one corner of the panel. Satin-stitch around the star with contrasting thread.

7. To hem the backing, fold one 36" edge 1 1/2" to the wrong side, fold again, and press. Topstitch along the first fold.

8. Evenly space the five female snap sections along this inside hem; sew in place. Sew the corresponding male snap sections to the inside bottom edge of the duvet front.

9. Layer the duvet backing and front right sides together, hemmed edges matching. Sew around the three unfinished edges, making a 1/2" seam.

10. Fold each 8" ribbon in half and stitch to the seam allowance at the two top corners and 3" from the bottom corners. Sew a plastic ring to each corner of the comforter. Tie the ribbons through the rings to hold the comforter in place.

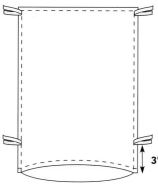

3"

Bundle of Love Bunting

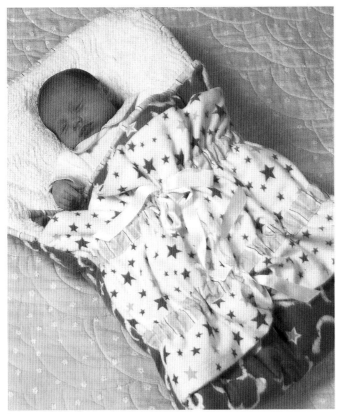

Inspired by a Margaret Peters design, this machine-washable bunting uses chenille on the inside next to baby's skin and flannel on the outside for the caretaker. Inside ties hold the flaps secure and prevent baby from wiggling through; 18" x 39".

Supplies

Note: Allow extra fabric for matching plaids, large prints, or one-way designs.

Flannel: 5/8 yard for outer fabric back

Chenille: 5/8 yard for lining

Contrasting fabric: 5/8 yard for flaps

Satin ribbon, 1/2" wide: 3 yards

Fabric for ribbon casing: 1/8 yard

Novelty braid or ribbon, 1 1/4" wide: 1 1/2 yards

Piping, 1/2" wide: 1 3/4 yards

Batting, 10-ounce: 18" x 39" rectangle

Matching thread

Pearl cotton #8 in contrasting color for tying

Embroidery needle

Cutting

Flannel and chenille:
    Cut one 19" x 40" rectangle from each fabric for outer back and lining.
Contrasting fabric:
    Cut two 21" x 14 1/2" rectangles for flaps.
Satin ribbon:
    Cut four 18" lengths for outside ties.
    Cut four 7 1/2" lengths for inside ties.
Fabric for ribbon casing:
    Cut four 1 1/2" x 11" strips.

Assembly

1. Lay the flannel back and chenille lining pieces right sides together; pin. Fold in half lengthwise, edges matching. Using a saucer as a template, draft and cut a rounded corner through both layers. Trim the batting to match.

2. Fold each flap in half crosswise, right side in, to make a piece 10 1/2" x 14 1/2". Stitch along each 10 1/2" edge, making a 1/2" seam. Clip the corners and turn right side out.

3. Fold in both long edges and one short edge of each casing strip 1/4", fold in again, and topstitch, to make narrow hem. Lay the two flaps flat, in mirror image. Position two casings on each flap, 3" from the top and bottom edges with finished edges parallel and aligned. Topstitch the long edges of each casing. Use a safety pin to draw an 18" ribbon through each casing, until 1/4" extends beyond the raw edge.

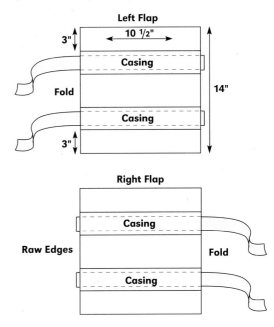

4. Lay the flannel back flat, right side up, with the rounded corners at the top. Lay the right flap on top, casing side down, 9 1/2" from the top; align the raw edges on the right. Place a 7 1/2" ribbon tie on the raw edge 1 1/2" below the top edge of the flap. Baste the flap and ribbon in place along the raw edge. Baste a second ribbon tie 4 1/2" from the bunting's bottom edge. Repeat to baste the left flap and ties to the left edge.

5. Using a zipper foot, sew piping around the top edge, turning in the raw edges at each end.

6. Place the chenille lining on top, right side down. Stitch 1/2" seam allowance all around, starting and stopping 1/2" from the bottom edge; leave the bottom open. Turn right side out and press.

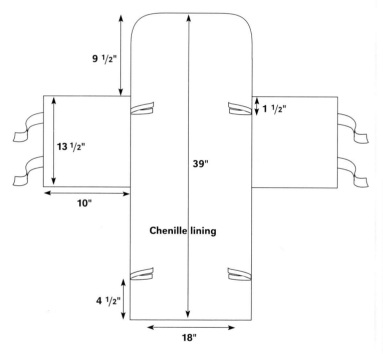

7. Put the batting inside the bunting. Fold the raw bottom edges 1/2" to the inside and stitch. Sew piping along this edge so it will show when the bundle is folded up.

8. Lay the bunting flat and open the flaps. Using pearl cotton and an embroidery needle, tie the layers together 2 1/2" below the center top (refer to a basic quiltmaking book for details). Measure down another 4" and make two ties 4" in from the side seams. Measure down another 4" and make another single tie. Continue as established until the entire bunting is tied.

9. To use the bunting, fold up the bottom and tie the inside ribbons, and then fold over and tie the front flaps. Pull the ribbons snug to gather the flaps.

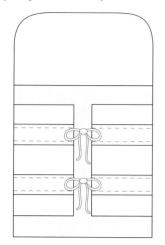

Fish Mobile

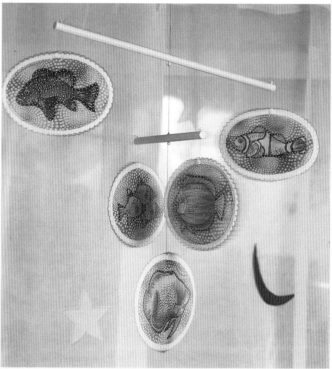

Designed and made by Betty Ann Watts, using individual fish motifs cut from Jennifer Sampou fabric; see Sources for details.

Supplies

Blue fabric: 1/4 yard for background

Fish print fabric: Enough to harvest 10 fish motifs

Bias picot trim: 2 1/2 yards

Pony beads, small: 11

Fusible web (paper-backed): 1/2 yard

Fleece or thin batting: 1/4 yard

Wooden dowel, 1/4" diameter: 20"

White spray paint

Drill and small drill bit

Small plastic curtain ring

Blue #5 pearl cotton

Embroidery needle

Fray Check™

Template plastic

Teflon pressing sheet

Assembly

1. Make one circle template and two oval templates (page 99). Following the manufacturer's instructions, mark four circles, four small ovals, and two large ovals on fusible web's paper backing. Fuse to the wrong side of the background fabric. Cut out the pieces, but do not remove the paper backing.

2. Cut two circles, two small ovals, and one large oval from fleece or batting. Trim 1/4" from the edge of each batting piece all around.

3. Knot a 10" length of pearl cotton through a bead, then tack the bead to the batting so the thread hangs loose.

4. Fuse a piece of webbing to the wrong side of each fish motif. Cut out each fish and fuse to a background piece.

5. Remove the paper backing from the background circles and ovals. Place two matching shapes wrong sides together, making sure each fish faces up. Sandwich the batting in between so the hanger comes out the top. Place the sandwich inside a folded Teflon sheet, and fuse the edges all around. (The Teflon sheet will protect your iron and ironing board from any oozing adhesive.)

6. Sew the bias picot trim around the edge of each circle or oval.

7. Cut dowel into one 13 1/2" and one 6 1/2" piece. Spray-paint each piece white. Let dry. Drill two tiny holes side by side in the middle and a hole 1/4" from each end of both dowels.

8. Fold a 60" length of pearl cotton in half. Knot the looped end through a curtain ring. Thread each free end through the two middle holes in the long dowel, then through one pony bead in a figure-eight arrangement.

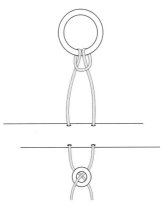

9. Draw up the threads to the desired length and tie a single knot against the bead on the underside of the dowel. Attach the short dowel 3" to 4" below and tie off in the same way. Do not cut the thread; you may need to make adjustments further on.

10. Thread each small oval hanger through an end hole of the longer dowel. Adjust the thread length to 1", and tie off with a bead on top of the dowel. Repeat to join the two circles to the short dowel. Tie the large oval's hanger to the bead under the short dowel.

11. Hang the mobile, check the balance, and adjust the threads as necessary. Secure all the knots with Fray Check. Let dry, then snip off thread ends.

Star Bright Painted Ceiling

Designed and painted by Jennifer Sampou using Benjamin Moore paints; see Sources.

This painting technique combines glazing and sponge stamping to transfer large patterns quickly. Paint the ceiling and the top 4" of the wall blue and let dry. Mix glaze and white paint in 1:1 ratio—you'll need about 3 cups total to cover 150 square feet. Using a large sponge, rub the glaze mixture over the blue area for a soft, colorwashed effect. This ceiling's textured surface appeared even more three-dimensional once the glaze was worked in. Paint the tangerine border with a 7" paint roller; you can work freehand or chalk in a guideline. If you place two different tangerine paints in the paint tray, swirl twice around with paint stick, and then load the roller, you'll achieve a dual-color look with hardly any effort.

To make your star stamps, draw a few 5-pointed stars on paper (ours measure 7", 8 1/2", and 10") and then cut your shapes from large car wash sponges. Moisten the sponge with yellow acrylic craft paint, blot off the excess, and carefully press the sponge onto the ceiling to transfer the star image. Continue stamping a variety of stars until the sky looks complete. Use the edge of a kitchen sponge to add tangerine shading. Paint the turquoise scrolls freehand with an artist's brush so each one is slightly different. Stamp the lime green dots with a 2" circle sponge.

Painted Chest

Painted by Jennifer Sampou.

To resurrect an old piece of furniture, you'll need sandpaper and elbow grease. Begin by removing all the old hardware and filling in the holes with wood filler if they don't match your new hardware. If the paint is already peeling off in sheets, help it along with a flat-bladed scraper. Use an electric sander on large flat surfaces, such as dresser tops and drawer fronts. It is not crucial to sand off all the paint, but do try to create as smooth a surface as possible. Wipe up the residual dust with a tack cloth.

We suggest applying an oil-base primer followed by two coats of semigloss latex. Remove drawers and doors and, if possible, paint each surface face up to avoid drips. Use a brush to paint furniture (a roller will leave a bumpy texture), and apply each coat with precision and care. Follow the manufacturer's recommendations to allow the proper drying time, and sand in between the coats using 150- or 220-grit sandpaper for a smooth-as-glass finish. You will be surprised how wonderful an old "hunk of junk" can look with a fresh coat of paint.

Shimmering
Tonight
s**t**A**r
b**R**ight

a**B**ove
my **R**oom
in the
Galaxy
t**H**ey are
Twinkling

—CHLÖE SCHMITZ, AGE 10

CAMPING OUT

Kids love camping. We can remember our folks piling all five of us in the Chevrolet Suburban and heading north to the mountains in New Hampshire. Camping meant fishing and swimming in icy rivers, cooking on an open fire, and staying up late to watch the stars come out.

Like a Paul Bunyan tall tale, everything about this youngster's year-round campsite is larger than life. Beefy buffalo plaids and jumbo rickrack accent the bedding, and the sturdy handmade wooden furniture, painted lake blue and forest green, has a bold, outdoorsy look. If sleeping in a bed seems too civilized (or if a friend spends the night), there's a fleece "buddy bag" with an oversized trout appliqué and huge sawtooth border. Need a bear hug? Two friendly companions lounging nearby are ready to oblige. The only thing missing is the mosquitoes!

Designer
Touches

Turn nooks and niches into special play areas. An elevated platform can become a stage for theatrical revues or make-believe tableaus, such as a teddy bear picnic. A colorful hand-hooked rug enlivens the nook and makes the floor more comfortable for sitting. Be sure to add lighting if the nook is dark.

Use matching colors to avoid an overly cluttered appearance. Here, a brown beanbag chair visually "disappears" when set on the mushroom-toned floor.

Camp Fire Stories

■ A triptych mural painted on canvas can be hung as a group or as individual panels, for a variety of display options. Unlike a mural that is painted directly on the wall, canvas panels are easy to take down and put up when the room is repainted or the furniture is rearranged. Suspending the panels from slender tree limbs instead of dowels highlights the room's back-to-nature theme.

■ Make rustic shelving from found objects. The bow of an old canoe was fitted with shelves to make a child-sized whatnot cabinet. The canoe is bolted to the wall so it won't topple over.

Designed and pieced by the authors using Robert Kaufman and Jennifer Sampou fabrics, see Sources for details;
layered and tied by Mabeth Oxenreider; 63 ¹/₂" x 87".

BLUE AND RED FLANNEL LOG CABIN QUILT

Young campers will love snuggling under this Log Cabin quilt made of soft, warm cotton flannels and other sporty fabrics. Reds, blues, greens, and browns combine in the familiar block design, while the unique bold sizing makes the piecing go extra-fast. Each block is different, but a beefy red buffalo plaid ties them all together. The quilt layers are hand-tied with yarn for a fast finish.

Supplies

Red plaid flannel: 2 3/8 yards for sashing and borders

Red check or plaid flannels: Twelve 6 1/2" squares of 4 to 6 different flannels for the block centers

Blues: 2 yards total of seven or eight different cotton prints for blocks

Browns: 1 yard total of seven or eight different cotton prints for blocks

Greens: 1/2 yard total of two or three different cotton prints for blocks

Plaid flannel: 5 1/4 yards for the backing

Dark blue: 5/8 yard for binding; cut 2 1/8"-wide strips.

Batting: 68" x 91"

Red yarn and dark blue yarn

Large-eyed embroidery needle

Cutting

Cotton prints: Cut into strips 7/8" to 3" wide, using blues for the wider widths.

Red plaid flannel:

  Cut eight 3"-wide strips. Piece as necessary to cut eight 16 1/2" vertical sashing strips and three 53 1/2" horizontal sashing strips.

  Cut three 8"-wide strips. Piece as necessary to cut two 53 1/2" lengths for top and bottom borders.

  Cut five 5 1/2"-wide strips. Piece as necessary to cut two 87" lengths for side borders.

Assembly

Make 1/4" seams throughout.

1. Sew any narrow cotton print strip to one edge of a red flannel center block, right sides together. Trim off the excess strip even with the block edge. Press the seam toward the strip. Working counterclockwise around the block, add strips 2, 3, and 4 using the same fabric. Change to a new cotton print and add strips 5, 6, 7, and 8.

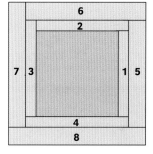

2. Continue adding strips in groups of four around the center block for four to six rounds or until the block measures 16 1/2" square; use the wider blue strips toward the outer edge of the block. Repeat to make twelve blocks total.

3. Arrange blocks in four rows of three. Join each group of three blocks with two red vertical sashing strips. Press the seams toward the sashing. Join the four rows with three red horizontal sashing strips; press toward the sashing. Add the red top and bottom borders; press toward the borders. Add the red side borders and press.

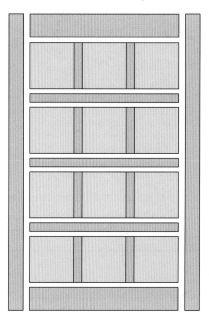

Quilting

1. Layer the quilt top, batting, and back. Baste with safety pins.

2. Tie the quilt using a large-eyed embroidery needle and yarn (refer to a basic quiltmaking book for details). Use red yarn in the borders and sashing and blue yarn in the blocks. Follow the batting manufacturer's recommendation for spacing the ties.

3. Bind to finish.

Camp Sheets

Designed by Jennifer Sampou; stitched by Lyn Lackey of Bernina® using Isacord thread, color #3544; see Sources.

We used a computer to embroider these one-of-a-kind designs. Use our images (page 105) or draw your own. Scan the images into your computer, then manually digitize each picture using appropriate software. Follow the manufacturer instructions for your particular machine to digitize the images and select different stitch widths for the finer details and heavier outlines in your images. We used Artista Designer Software Version 2.0, the Artista 180

Sewing Computer, and Isacord thread. When you are satisfied with the on-screen version, send the image onto your computer sewing machine for stitching out. Think of it as using your sewing machine as a printer!

The stitching is done just like in any other machine embroidery project. Secure the area to be embroidered in a medium-sized hoop with a soft tear-away stabilizer underneath. Our images are stitched through a single layer of fabric just beyond the sheet's double-folded hem. To avoid "smashing" the finished embroidery, place it facedown on a terry towel and steam-press from the wrong side. For a finishing touch, sew on jumbo rickrack, using the existing hem topstitching as a guideline. You will need 3 yards of rickrack to trim one twin flat sheet and two pillowcases.

Buddy Bag

Designed by the authors; made by Carolyn Schmitz; 32" x 65".

Supplies

Use 60"-wide fleece, 45"-wide flannel.

Hunter green fleece: 2 yards

Navy blue fleece: 2 yards

Red fleece: 3/8 yard

Plaid flannel: 1 yard for the fish motif and binding

Ecru 4-ply yarn: 1 skein

Large-eyed embroidery needle

Cutting

Hunter green fleece:

Cut four 16 1/2" x 33" rectangles.

Navy blue fleece:

Cut four 16 1/2" x 33" rectangles.

Red fleece:

Cut two 5 1/2"-wide strips. Piece as necessary to cut one 65" strip and one 32" strip.

Plaid flannel:

Cut one fish appliqué (pages 102 and 103)

Cut seven 2"-wide strips for binding. Piece as necessary to make 255" of binding.

Assembly

1. Set up machine with a walking foot and narrow zigzag stitch; these will allow a more flexible seam that will stretch with the fleece when a child crawls in and out of the bag.

2. Sew each green rectangle to a blue rectangle right sides together on one long edge, making 1/2" seam. Press seam open. Sew these units together in pairs to make two Four-Patch panels for the bag front and back.

3. Center the fish appliqué on one Four-Patch panel; pin or baste. Zigzag edges all around. Thread needle with yarn and work blanket stitch around edge, spacing stitches 1/2" apart for a rustic appearance.

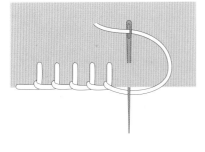

4. Make the sawtooth border template (page 103). Lay 32" red fleece strip flat, align the template at one end, and mark the first sawtooth. Reposition the template and mark the second sawtooth. Repeat to mark a cutting line with four sawtooth points. In the same way, mark nine sawtooth points on the 65" strip. Cut each strip in half on the zigzag line to yield two border strips. Trim off the extra fabric from each strip.

5. Lay the fish appliqué panel (bag front) face up. Position sawtooth borders on panel, flush with outside edges. Baste the outside edges. Zigzag the sawtooth edges and work blanket stitch, as for fish in step 3.

6. Using a 1/2" seam, bind the top edge and 14" down one side of the bag front. Bind the bag back to correspond.

7. Place the bag front and back wrong sides together. Stitch the raw edges together to create a bag with roomy L-shaped opening at the top. Bind the raw edges on three sides, folding in the excess binding strip at each end. Reinforce the base of the 14" opening by sewing a bar tack (a wide satin stitch) through all the layers.

8. To store the bag, fold it in half lengthwise, roll it up from one end, and wrap with a bungee cord.

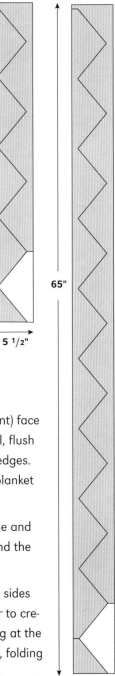

32"

5 1/2"

65"

5 1/2"

Designed and made by Carolyn Schmitz; middle panel, 36" x 36"; side panels, 21" x 36" each. See Sources to order canvas.

Triptych Mural

If you or someone you know has a flair for painting, try this fun canvas wall art. Cut a 38" square of canvas for the middle panel and two 23" x 38" pieces for the flanking side panels. Fold under and glue the edges as you would a floorcloth (see Family Tree Floorcloth, page 19, step 1). To prepare the canvas for painting, apply an acrylic primer and let it dry overnight. Paint your picture on the canvas using acrylic craft paint or artist's acrylics. Be sure the paint extends onto the edges of each panel. Let dry overnight. To hang the triptych, use a holepunch or awl to punch a hole at the top corner of each panel. Thread a strip of rawhide through each hole. Tie each panel to its own stick.

"**My lumber camp was the LARGEST CAMP in this country. The bunkhouses stretched for FIVE MILES in all directions and each had five tiers of bunks, one above the other.**"

—A PAUL BUNYAN TALL TALE

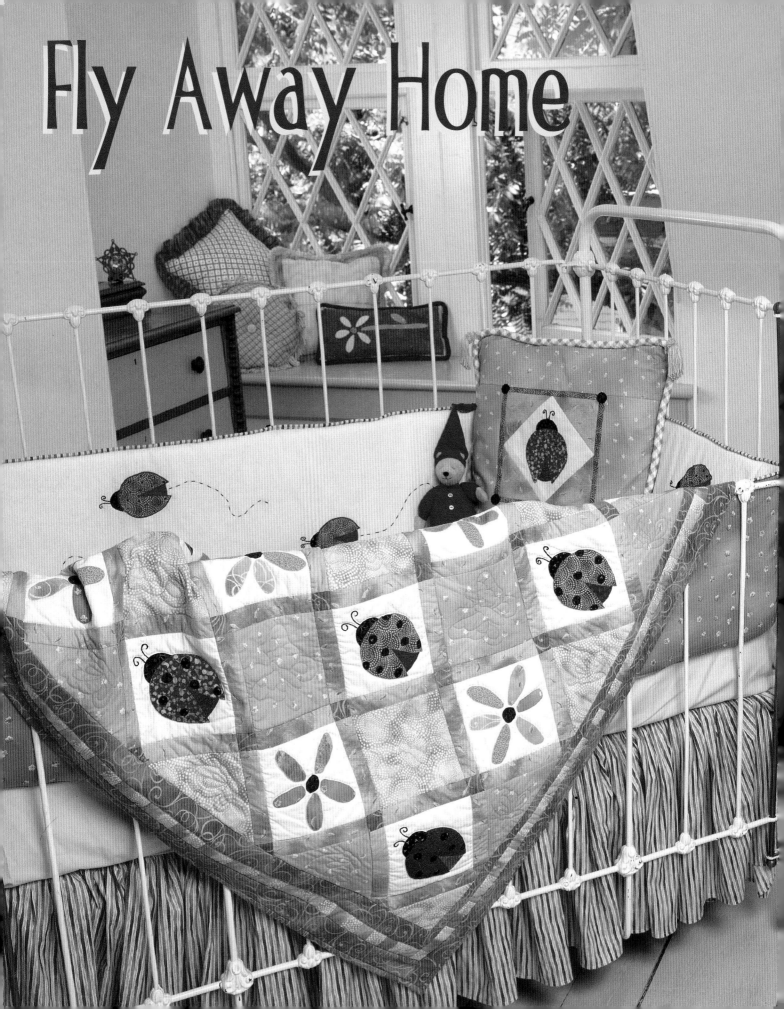

Fly Away Home

he butterfly quilt first caught Carolyn's eye as she was racing to pick up her children from school. It was draped in a sidewalk display in front of her favorite antiques shop, looking bold and crude in a fresh, simple way. She purchased the 1940s era quilt for a twin bed and worked from there to develop the garden theme for the entire bedroom. The ladybug, fun and playful with her red cloak and black spots, was a natural motif choice for baby's quilt. Like a toddler who's off and running, more ladybugs buzz along on the bumper pads, leaving behind little trails of stitching to indicate their flight paths.

Once you've established a room's ambiance, cosmetic improvements practically suggest themselves. The old floor boards in this attic bedroom were stained and beyond refinishing, but two shades of green paint quickly and affordably transformed them into a grassy "lawn." The same green paint applied to the dormer nook leads the eye up to the diamond-paned windows and to the green foliage in the real garden just beyond.

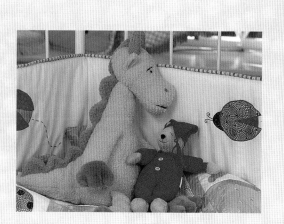

Designer Touches

Go with a palette you love! For a bright, offbeat combination, try analogous colors like marigold, tangerine, and strawberry complemented by grass green. Such a jubilant mix requires large doses of soft white to relieve the color intensity and give the eye a resting spot.

A crib and twin bed arrangement works perfectly for baby and an older sibling or when you need the nursery to double as a guest room.

Ladybug! Ladybug! Fly away home

■ Window seats become even more inviting when cushioned with throw pillows. For a coordinated look, sew the pillows from your leftover quiltmaking fabrics.

■ Horizontal stripes painted above the baseboard or below the cornice help set off these architectural moldings from the wall. Use this simple painting technique much as you would a wallpaper border to avoid a "bare white walls" look.

■ Low-mounted hooks encourage toddlers to hang up their own things, especially if you splurge on novelty designs. Avoid sharp hooks, and mount the hooks above the child's eye level.

■ Floors don't have to be brown. Paint or carpeting can color a floor any hue you want to help fill out a room's palette. An infant's room receives little foot traffic, so light colors are not impractical.

Designed by the authors using Jennifer Sampou fabrics, see Sources for details; pieced and quilted by Mabeth Oxenreider; 44 1/2" x 52 1/2".

Ladybug, Ladybug Quilt

aby's ladybug crib quilt mimics the diamond-set blocks of Carolyn's older, more mellow butterfly quilt, but the addition of sashing prevents a strict cookie cutter interpretation. Vivid analogous colors—marigold, tangerine, strawberry, and flamingo—create a hot harmony of color that's cooled off with garden green. When viewed together, the quilts exhibit a charming "generation gap."

Supplies

Red and pink prints: Twenty scraps, at least 6" square, for ladybugs and flowers

Solid black: Scraps for ladybugs and flowers

Off-white: $3/4$ yard for background

Green #1: $2/3$ yard for alternate blocks, setting and corner triangle, and checkerboard border

Green #2: $1/2$ yard for alternate blocks, setting and corner triangles

Yellow-gold: 1 yard total; $3/4$ yard for sashing, $1/4$ yard for checkerboard border

Orange: $1 1/2$ yards for cornerstones, borders, and binding

Backing: $2 2/3$ yards

Batting: 49" x 57"

Fusible web (paper-backed): $1/2$ yard

Black #8 pearl cotton for embroidered details

Embroidery needle

Cutting

Off-white: Cut twenty 6" squares.

Greens #1 and #2: Cut six 6" squares from each green for 12 alternate blocks.

Cut two 9" squares from each green, then cut diagonally in each direction for 14 setting triangles.

Cut one $4 7/8$" square from each green, then cut diagonally in one direction for 4 corner triangles.

Green #1 only:

Cut four $1 1/2$"-wide strips for checkerboard border.

Yellow-gold: Cut fourteen $1 1/2$"-wide strips into eighty 6" strips for sashing.

Cut four $1 1/2$"-wide strips for checkerboard border.

Orange: Cut two $1 1/2$"-wide strips into 31 squares for cornerstones.

Cut five $2 3/4$" squares. Then cut diagonally in each direction for 18 cornerstone setting triangles.

Cut three $1 5/8$"-wide strips. Piece as necessary to cut two $46 1/2$" lengths for inner side borders.

Cut two 1" x $39 1/2$" strips for inner top and bottom borders.

Cut three 2"-wide strips. Piece as necessary to cut two $49 1/2$" lengths for the outer side borders.

Cut three 2"-wide strips. Piece as necessary to cut two $44 1/2$" outer top and bottom borders.

Reserve balance for binding; cut strips $2 1/4$" wide.

Assembly

1. Make the ladybug and flower templates (page 100). Mark the pieces for ten ladybugs and ten flowers on the paper backing of fusible web; group the pieces by color. Also mark a few extra flower petals. Following the manufacturer's instructions, fuse the pieces to the appropriate color fabrics and cut out.

2. Lay an off-white square on point. Arrange the pieces for one ladybug on it and fuse in place. Repeat to appliqué ten ladybug blocks. In the same way, appliqué ten flower blocks. Give some flowers six petals instead of five.

3. Satin-stitch around each motif with matching thread. Embroider each ladybug's antennae in stem stitch with black pearl cotton.

4. Sew a yellow-gold sashing strip to the top right and lower left edges of each diamond block, right sides together. Press the seam toward the strip.

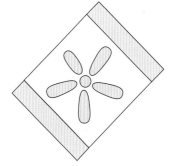

5. Arrange the off-white and green blocks in a diagonal set, alternating the ladybugs and flowers with the two different green blocks; see the quilt photo on page 62 and the diagram below. Add the remaining yellow-gold sashing strips and the orange cornerstone squares. Fill in the edges with the green and orange triangles.

6. Sew the orange cornerstone setting triangles, yellow-gold sashing strips, and orange cornerstone squares into rows. Press seams toward the sashing strips.

7. Sew the off-white and green blocks together in rows, adding a green setting triangle at each end. (Note that Rows 4 and 5 will have a green setting triangle at one end only.) Press seams toward the sashing strips. As each row is sewn, return it to its place in the layout.

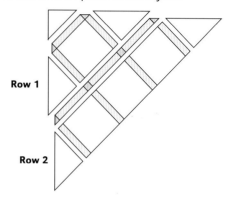

Row 1

Row 2

8. Join the block and sashing rows. Add the four green corner triangles. Press all the seams in the same direction.

9. Square up the edges, allowing for a 1/4" seam allowance all around.

10. Attach the orange inner side borders. Press seams toward the border. Attach the orange inner top and bottom borders (note that they are narrower); press.

11. Sew the green and yellow-gold strips together, alternating the colors. Press seams toward the green strips. Cut the strip-set unit into 1 1/2"-wide checkerboard strips.

1 1/2" 1 1/2"

12. Sew the checkerboard strips end to end to make two 47 1/2" lengths for the side borders and two 41 1/2" lengths for the top and bottom borders. Press seams toward the green squares.

13. Attach the side checkerboard borders, then the top and bottom borders. Press seams toward the inner border.

14. Attach the outer side borders, then the outer top and bottom borders. Press seams toward the outer border.

Quilting

Layer quilt backing, batting, and top. Baste with safety pins. Stitch-in-the-ditch around each block, cornerstone, and border. Quilt around the outside of each appliqué. Machine-quilt the design of your choice (we used butterflies) in the setting squares and triangles. Bind to finish.

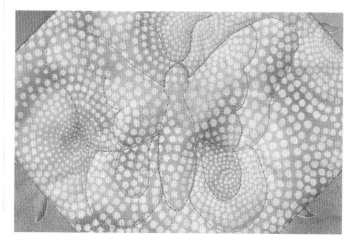

Ladybug Bumper Pad

Designed and made by Jennifer Sampou.

Supplies

Fabric #1: 1 3/4 yards off-white for inside bumper

Fabric #2: 1 3/4 yards medium red print for outside bumper

Fabric for piping: 5/8 yard red check

Batting, 10-ounce, 48"-wide: 1 5/8 yards

Ribbon: 6 1/4 yards, or 3/8 yard coordinating fabric, for ties

Cording for piping: 4 1/2 yards

Black #8 pearl cotton

Embroidery needle

Fusible web (paper-backed): 1 yard

Assembly

1–4. Same as the Basic Bumper Pad instructions steps 1–4 on page 88.

5. Photocopy the ladybug pattern (page 100) at 85%. Prepare 12 fusible appliqués, following the manufacturer's instructions. Fuse the ladybugs in random positions to the fabric #1 piece. Machine–satin-stitch around each ladybug with matching thread. Using black pearl cotton, hand-embroider each ladybug's antennae in stem stitch, add French knot dots to her coat, and add a running stitch trail behind her.

6. Make 4 1/2 yards of red check piping. Add piping to the top edge, as per basic instructions step 5 (refer to a basic sewing or quiltmaking book for more details).

7. Continue with basic instructions steps 7, 8, and 9.

Ladybug Pillow

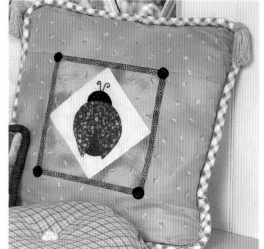

Designed and made by Jennifer Sampou using Jennifer Sampou fabrics, see Sources for details; 16" x 16".

Supplies

Off-white fabric: 6" square for appliqué background

Yellow print: Two 4 3/4" squares

Reds: Scraps of three different prints for ladybug appliqué and narrow border

Black: Scraps for the ladybug and corner circles

Green print: 3/8 yard for wide border

Pink check: 1/2 yard for bias piping

Pink print: 3/8 yard for pillow back

14" zipper

Cotton/polyester cording, 1/2" diameter: 2 yards

Tassels: 4

Pearl cotton #8 in black and red

Embroidery needle

Fusible web scraps

Pillow form, 18" square

Cutting

Yellow print: Cut the squares diagonally in one direction.

One red print: Cut one 7/8"-wide strip into two 8 1/4" lengths and two 9" lengths for narrow border.

Green print: Cut two 5"-wide strips. From each strip, cut one 9" length and one 18" length.

Pinks: Cut one 9 1/2"-wide strip into two 18" pieces for pillow back. Cut a continuous bias strip 2 1/2" wide x 72" long for the piping (refer to a basic sewing or quiltmaking book for details).

Assembly

All seams are $1/4$" unless otherwise noted.

1. To assemble the appliqué background, stitch two yellow triangles to opposite sides of the 6" off-white square. Press the seams toward the triangles. Stitch the remaining two yellow triangles to the other two edges.

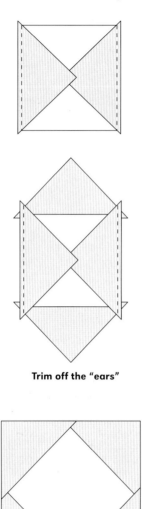

Trim off the "ears"

2. Sew the 8 $1/4$" red border strips to the top and bottom of the square, then sew the 9" strips to the sides. Press seams toward border. Sew the 9" green border strips to the sides, then sew the 18" strips to the top and bottom. Press seams toward the green border.

3. Cut and fuse one ladybug appliqué to the off-white diamond, as for the Ladybug Quilt steps 1 and 2. Cut and fuse 4 penny-sized black circles to the corners of the red border.

4. Blanket-stitch around the ladybug with red pearl cotton. Backstitch the antennae and blanket-stitch around the corner circles with black.

5. Place the pillow backs right sides together. Baste a $1/2$" seam along one 18" edge. Press the seam open. Install a zipper along this seam, following the manufacturer's instructions.

6. Using a zipper foot, make piping from cording and pink bias strip. Machine-baste the piping to the pillow front just inside the $1/2$" seam line (refer to a basic sewing or quilt-making book for details).

7. Pin the pillow back and front right sides together. Partially open the zipper. Now stitch a $1/2$" seam all around, as close to the piping as possible. Turn the cover right side out. Tack a tassel to each corner. Insert the pillow form and zip closed.

Daisy Pillow

Designed and made by Jennifer Sampou; 8 $1/2$" x 17".

Supplies

Pink: $1/3$ yard for background
Pink stripe: $1/8$ yard for border
White: $1/3$ yard, cut into one 9 $1/2$" x 18" piece for backing
Scraps for flower, stem, and leaf appliqués
Red print: $1/2$ yard for bias piping
Cotton/polyester cording, $1/2$" diameter: 1 $1/2$ yards
Polyfill for stuffing
Machine embroidery thread to match appliqués

Pink: Cut one 8" x 16 1/2" rectangle.

Pink stripe:

Cut two 1 1/4"-wide strips. From each strip, cut one 16 1/2" length and one 9 1/2" length for border.

Red print:

Cut two 2 1/2"-wide strips. Piece together and cut a 54" length for the piping.

Assembly

All seams are 1/4" unless otherwise noted.

1. Sew the side borders to the pink background, then sew top and bottom borders. Press after each step.

2. Cut and fuse one flower appliqué (page 100) to the pink background diamond, as for the Ladybug Quilt steps 1 and 2. Satin-stitch around the motif with matching machine embroidery thread.

3. Using a zipper foot, make and attach the piping, as for Ladybug Pillow step 6.

4. Pin the pillow back and front right sides together. Using a zipper foot, stitch a 1/2" seam around three sides as close to piping as possible. Turn right side out, stuff with polyfill, and hand-sew closed.

Picket Fence Headboard

You will need eleven pickets, each about 52" long x 3 1/2" wide. Measuring from the top down, saw nine pickets into graduated lengths: one 50", two 46", two 42", two 38", and two 34". Measuring the two remaining pickets from the bottom up, saw two 41 1/2" lengths for the crossboards. (Reserve the two leftover picket tops for the Bug Hooks project.) Arrange the pickets side by side on a flat surface, 3/4" apart and lower edges aligned. Position the crossboards 1" or 5 1/2" if bolting to bed frame and 27" from the bottom edge. Secure the crossboards to each picket with screws. Prime and paint the headboard as desired, sanding in between coats. For a weathered look, sand with 150-grit sandpaper after final coat. Bolt to wall or bed frame.

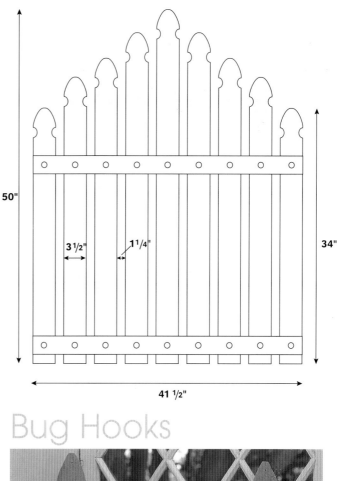

Bug Hooks

Made by Carolyn Schmitz; 14" x 28".

Saw two picket tops to a 14" length. Saw a board 28" long (or the desired length) for the crossboard. Lay the pickets flat, then position the crossboard on them at a right angle as shown. Secure with two screws on each side. Prime and paint the rack, sanding in between coats. Attach the hooks to the crossboard. Mount using nails or screws.

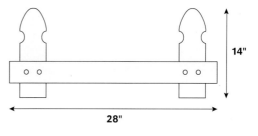

Butterfly Light

Designed and made by Wendy Neale to fit an electric Welcome Light.

You'll need 10 to 12 small pictures of butterflies, cut from a découpage design book, giftwrap, or a similar source, for this project. Transfer the lampshade pattern (page 101) to posterboard. Lightly draft the lines connecting the top and bottom edge scallops, then paint every other section for a striped effect. Cut out the lampshade. Glue on the butterfly cutouts at random. Overlap and glue the side tab, holding in place with your fingers or clothespins until the glue has set. Use a chandelier clip to attach the shade to a purchased Welcome Light (see Sources).

Painted Baseboard and Floor Stripes

Baseboard stripes painted by Carolyn Schmitz using craft acrylics. Floor paints from Pratt & Lambert; see Sources.

To highlight a baseboard, draft a chalk line on the wall 2" above the baseboard. Mask off the surrounding area with blue painter's tape. Paint the stripe using marigold acrylic craft paint. Let dry 30 minutes. Brush on a mix of cherry and marigold paint to add random shading, wiping with a clean, damp rag if the color gets too heavy. Let dry 4 hours. Repeat to paint a 1"-wide cherry stripe above the marigold stripe; highlight with a marigold/cherry mix.

On an old floor, use the planks themselves to determine the stripe width. If the planks are narrow, use two or three for each color stripe. Uneven widths add to the charm. Apply the base coat to entire floor and let dry. For the glaze, mix equal parts of oil-base paint, oil-base glazing liquid, and mineral spirits. Brush the glaze onto alternate planks to create the stripes. For a more subtle contrast, wipe off the some of the glaze. Let dry. A protective finish is not necessary on this painted floor.

"One day I caught a ladybug.

I gave her a new home.

She liked her new home.

She came back for dinner

every night."

—GREGORY VOGT, AGE 10

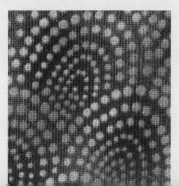

Yellow Ribbons

If picking a color scheme makes you nervous, try this easy recipe: a pastel color teamed with white. We began by painting the walls golden yellow and washing over them with milky white glaze to lighten and soften the color. Yellow ribbons were painted over this hushed background. Bows and ribbons are a romantic, feminine image for a baby girl and, as painted motifs, are easy to adapt to the available wall space. Ribbon streamers can be painted to wind around door or window frames, frame a crib or dresser, or even trail off onto the ceiling. Here, the ribbons support a graceful swag of daisies—a motif inspired by the pretty window sheers.

For more fresh-as-a-daisy appeal, we chose simple, unfussy furnishings. The old paint-worn cupboard is serviceable, and its tall, narrow profile doesn't crowd the small space. A floral hooked rug provides serenity and comfort, while a Victorian armchair, reupholstered in white fabric, invites lingering near the crib. Our favorite aspect of the bedding is the unique use of tulle, sure to delight any budding ballerina.

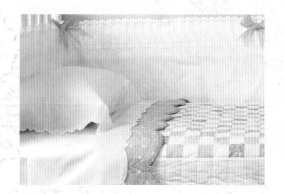

Designer Touches

Angle the furniture to face out into the room, for a pleasing view as you enter. A room can feel dull and lifeless when cribs and cupboards are backed into the corners, but arranging them around a rug creates a warm, inviting play area for a toddler. An old kitchen cupboard adapts beautifully to the nursery. Pieces that offer both open display shelves and closed storage are especially useful.

Sunshine
Buttercup
Lemon drop

Fine details such as embroidered linen and hand-tied bows add elegant, feminine touches to a little girl's room.

Use glazes to add depth, interest, and softness to ordinary flat wall colors. A glaze coat will also let you alter an existing color without having to repaint the whole room. For instance, if a room is currently white, you can glaze over in any color, dramatically changing the room for a lot less time and money.

Whimsically patterned sheers look fresh and spontaneous teamed with a traditional quilt and enhance a room's ambiance by softly filtering the natural light. The more obvious choice—white eyelet, to match the bumper pads—is safe, but far less interesting. Shades discreetly mounted underneath provide darkness and privacy when needed.

Designed by Jennifer Sampou using Jennifer Sampou fabrics (see Sources for details); pieced and quilted by Mabeth Oxenreider; 39 $\frac{1}{2}$" x 51 $\frac{1}{2}$".

classic two-tone crib quilt creates a sunny mood with its checkerboard of buttery yellow fabrics. To soften the quilt's sharp, crisp geometry, we added a wide white border and scalloped edge all around. The yellow scallops ribboning the border are easy to add. Simply fuse them in place and zigzag the edges by machine.

Supplies

Yellow prints: 5 yards total: 1/8 yard each of seven to eight different prints for center panel, 1/2 yard for swag, 1 yard for binding, 2 1/2 yards for backing

Off-white fabric: 2 yards for center panel and borders

Fusible web (paper-backed): 1/2 yard

Batting: 44" x 56"

Cutting

Yellow prints:

Cut one or two 2"-wide strips from each center panel fabric into 2" squares for a total of 213 squares.

Cut a continuous bias strip 2 1/8" wide x 270" long for binding (refer to a basic sewing or quiltmaking book for details).

Off-white fabric:

Cut eleven 2"-wide strips into 2" squares for a total of 212 squares.

Cut six 7 1/4"-wide strips for border. Piece as necessary to cut two 56 1/2" strips for side borders and two 44 1/2" strips for top and bottom borders.

Assembly

1. Referring to the quilt photo, opposite, arrange the yellow and white squares on a design board or wall in a checkerboard pattern (25 squares x 17 squares). Make sure each corner square is yellow.

2. Sew the squares together in rows. Press the seams toward the yellow squares.

3. Sew the rows together, pressing all the seams in the same direction.

4. Lay the checkerboard panel flat, right side up. Place the top border strip along the top edge, right sides together, so the strip overhangs the panel 9 1/2" at each end; pin. Stitch together, starting and stopping 1/4" from each corner of the panel. Join the remaining border strips in the same way. Miter the corners (refer to a basic quiltmaking book for more details).

5. Make swag templates A, B, and C (page 104). Mark ten top and bottom A swags, fourteen side B swags, and four corner C swags on the paper backing of fusible web. Label, fuse to yellow fabric, and cut out.

6. Arrange the swags on the quilt top approximately 4" beyond the pieced checkerboard; center each corner swag on the miter line. Adjust up or down where necessary to fit. Fuse in place. Sew a narrow open zigzag stitch around each swag.

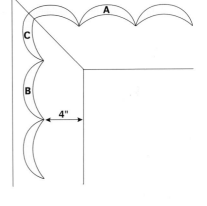

Quilting

1. Layer the quilt top, batting, and backing. Baste with safety pins.

2. Quilt the center panel with an allover design (such as Amish Wave, used here). Stitch-in-the-ditch around the center panel. On the border, stitch short parallel lines 1 1/2" apart from the center panel out to the quilt edge, jumping over the swags. Outline-quilt each swag.

3. Measure 1 1/4" beyond the swag to mark a scallop edge all around. Do not cut. Place the edge of the bias binding along the marked line, right sides together; stitch 1/4" from bias edge. Trim the excess fabric and batting. Fold the binding to the back and hand-sew in place.

Eyelet Bumper Pad

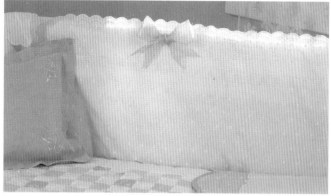

Designed and made by Jennifer Sampou.

Follow the Basic Bumper Pad instructions on page 88. Choose an eyelet with a decorative edge and cut the panels on the lengthwise grain; you will need to adjust the yardage requirements accordingly. To finish the top edge, follow the Alternate Finish step 8. Then fold in the back seam allowance only and topstitch closed. Weave a yellow ribbon through the eyelet insertion. To avoid a choking hazard for baby, tack the yellow bows to the outside of the bumper pad.

Tulle Dust Ruffle

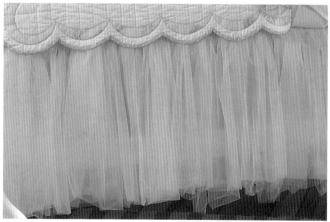

Designed by Anne Glazzard; made by Elsa Sampou.

Follow the Basic Dust Ruffle instructions on page 89. To make a skirt as full as the one shown, you will need 22 yards of 54"-wide tulle. Cut the tulle lengthwise into three strips. Layer the strips on top of each other and treat them as one piece. Cut two 135" lengths and two 260" lengths. Omit the hemming in step 1.

Yellow Ribbons Mural

This wall mural uses a combination of glazing and decorative painting. To glaze an average 10' x 12' room, mix 1 cup latex glaze, 1 cup paint, and 4 tablespoons water in a bucket. Measure carefully and keep a record of your recipe in case you need to mix more later. Starting at the top of the wall, brush on the glaze in a crisscross pattern, covering a 2' x 2' area. Immediately pounce the glaze with large sea sponge, moving and swirling it to create a cloudy texture that is somewhat even in distribution. You'll know the area is completed when you no longer see any of the original brush strokes and the base color appears luminous and softly blurred. Latex glaze dries fast, so work quickly. When you move on to the next 2' x 2' area, brush up to but not touching the previous edge and then blend into it with the sponge. Work from the top down so drips do not spoil your work.

To paint the ribbons, begin by drawing your design to size on tracing paper. Transfer the design to the wall, then turn the tracing over and make a mirror image transfer for the other half. Mix white and butterscotch acrylic craft paints together on a palette to create dark, medium, and light values. For a soft, transparent look, add some latex glazing liquid to the paints. Paint the entire ribbon with the middle value, then highlight and shade with light and dark values. When the paint is dry, use chalk to sketch in the daisy swag. Loosely paint the daisy petals and leaves using shades of white and green paint softened with glaze. Add the vine and yellow flower centers last.

Glazing and decorative mural painting by Carolyn Schmitz. Wall and trim paints from Benjamin Moore; see Sources.

"Yellow ribbons on my wall
Yellow ribbons in the hall
Yellow ribbons bright and fun
Yellow ribbons all night long."

—CHLÖE SCHMITZ, AGE 10

In Flight

Even the youngest children develop personal interests and passions. This room, designed for a budding pilot, contains toy airplanes, a brightly appliquéd airplane quilt, and other aviator novelties. The lofty cathedral ceiling gave us the idea for the painted walls. The pale blue mock wainscot works together with the darker blue carpeting to draw the eye downward and focus attention within four feet of the floor. This scale caters to the room's young occupant and helps make his living space more intimate and cozy. A soft, undulating white line painted between the yellow and blue wall areas suggests windy air currents.

As this room shows, a primary palette—red, yellow, and blue—doesn't need a lot of crayon-bright color to pack a punch. It is actually the paler shades on the wall that help float the palette around the room. Note, too, how the furniture's blonde wood tones read as yellow in this primary scheme. A final word of caution regarding red: use it sparingly, as it can be overbearing in abundance.

Designer Touches

⬛ Add a window view wherever you want. Start with an old multi-paned window from the salvage yard. Sand the wood to reveal the various painted undercoats, and replace the glass with Plexiglas. Staple the view of your choice to the back. We painted a cloud scene on foam core, but you could also use a poster.

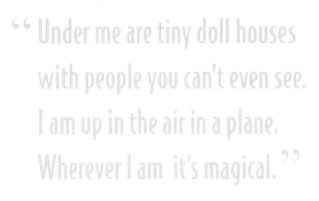

" Under me are tiny doll houses
with people you can't even see.
I am up in the air in a plane.
Wherever I am it's magical. "

—ANNA RIGBY WILSON, AGE 10

✿ Use a tie-on valance in a casual room.
The triangular panels in this valance look
like pennant flags flapping in the breeze.
Bright red ties anchor them to the exposed
rod, and each pennant ends in a drop made
of wooden beads and a jingle bell.

✿ Paint the backboards of bookcases
and hutches. Engine red paint makes a
colorful backdrop for toys and books on
the shelves of this maple bedroom set.

✿ Keep the room's theme in mind when
you shop for accessories. An airplane
hanging hook is much more fun than the
conventional type. Even lamps come in
novelty shapes.

Center appliqué and overall design by the authors using Jennifer Sampou fabrics (see Sources for details); assembled and quilted by Mabeth Oxenreider; 56 ½" x 85 ½".

In Flight Quilt

A n airplane quilt with a puppy dog pilot is the perfect taking off point for a young aviator's bedroom. To make the airplane, different, brightly colored fabric shapes are appliquéd to blue-and-white "cloud" fabric using paper-backed fusible web. A pieced pinwheel border continues the wind and flight theme. The wide stripes running down the face of the quilt make perfect airport runways for a fleet of toy planes.

Supplies

Medium blue print: $2/3$ yard for center motif background

Dark blue print: $1/4$ yard for center motif border

White chenille: $1/4$ yard for clouds

Bright red prints: Two different fat quarters for the airplane

Primary color prints: Assorted scraps for airplane details and Pinwheel blocks

Black: Scrap for puppy's nose and spots

White: Scrap for puppy

Light "cloud" fabric: $1 3/4$ yards for background and Pinwheel blocks

Blue-on-blue print: $3 1/2$ yards for background and outer border

Red mottled print: $3/8$ yard for the first inner border

Bright yellow print: $3/8$ yard for second inner border

Backing: 5 yards

Binding: $3/4$ yard of a second dark blue print

Batting, cotton: $1 3/4$ yards x 90"

Fusible web: 1 yard

Teflon pressing sheet

Cutting

Medium blue print:

Cut one $21 1/2$" square for center motif background.

Dark blue print:

Cut three $1 3/8$"-wide strips. Piece as necessary to cut two $21 1/2$" strips and two $23 1/4$" strips for center motif border.

Light "cloud" fabric:

Cut eight 6"-wide strips crosswise.

Cut two $2 7/8$"-wide strips into forty $2 7/8$" squares for 20 Pinwheel blocks.

Red mottled print:

Cut six $1 1/4$"-wide strips. Piece as necessary to cut two 39" strips and two 69" strips for first inner border.

Bright yellow print:

Cut six $1 1/4$"-wide strips. Piece as necessary to cut two $40 1/2$" strips and two $70 1/2$" strips for second inner border.

Primary color prints:

Cut forty $2 7/8$" squares for 20 Pinwheel blocks.

For each of the Pinwheel block borders, cut two 1" x $4 1/2$"-long strips and two 1" x $5 1/2$"-long strips.

Blue-on-blue print:

Cut six 6"-wide strips, crosswise.

Cut two $7 3/4$" x 85" outer side border strips, lengthwise.

Cut two $7 3/4$" x 42" outer top and bottom border strips, lengthwise.

Second dark blue print:

Cut eight $2 1/2$"-wide strips to be pieced for binding.

Assembly

1. Sew the light "cloud" strips right sides together in pairs, end to end, to make four long strips. Repeat to make three long blue-on-blue strips. Trim each strip to $67 1/2$" so the seam is in the middle. (The seam will be concealed by the airplane motif.) Press seam open.

2. Join these seven strips together on the long edges, starting and ending with a light "cloud" strip.

3. Add the red first inner border strips to the top and bottom edges; press toward the border. Add the red side border strips; press.

4. Repeat step 3 to add the yellow second inner border strips; press toward the red first inner borders.

5. Repeat step 3 to add the blue-on-blue outer border strips; press toward the blue-on-blue outer borders.

Airplane Appliqué

1. Lay the medium blue center motif background square on point on a flat surface. Cut three free-form clouds from white chenille. Arrange the clouds on the background so they overlap the top left, top right, and lower right edges as shown in the quilt photo (page 82). Pin in place. Secure cloud edges with a narrow zigzag.

2. Sew the two shorter dark blue border strips to opposite edges of the background square; press toward the border. Sew the longer strips to the two remaining edges; press. Fold under the raw edges 1/4" all around and press.

3. Transfer template pieces 1–27 (pages 105–108) to the paper backing of fusible web, grouping by color where possible. Following the manufacturer's instructions, fuse the pieces to the appropriate color fabrics and cut out.

4. Position the appliqués on the background. Fuse in place, following the numbered order and using the Teflon pressing sheet under the pieces that extend off the edges.

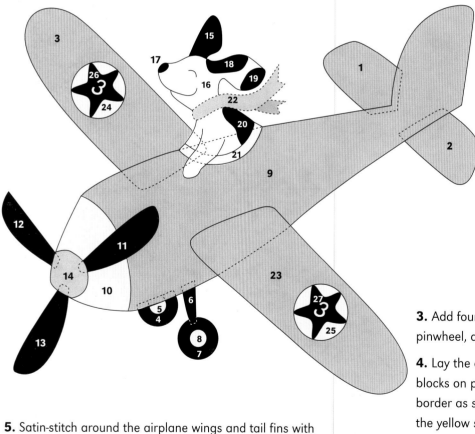

5. Satin-stitch around the airplane wings and tail fins with black thread.

6. Center the appliquéd piece on the quilt top; pin in place. Topstitch the outer edges of the dark blue border.

7. Fuse the extending wing tips, tail, and propeller blade to the quilt top. Satin-stitch or sew a narrow zigzag around each motif with matching thread.

Pinwheel Appliqué

1. Place a light "cloud" square and a primary color square right sides together. Draw a diagonal line from corner to corner. Machine-stitch 1/4" on each side of line, then cut on the line to make two half-square triangles. Press toward the primary color. Repeat to make four half-square triangles for each pinwheel (80 total).

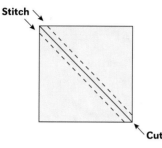

2. Sew four half-square triangles together to form a Pinwheel block. Press toward the darker fabric. Repeat to make 20 Pinwheel blocks.

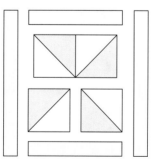

3. Add four primary color border strips to each pinwheel, as for Airplane Appliqué step 2.

4. Lay the quilt top flat. Arrange the Pinwheel blocks on point on the blue-on-blue outside border as shown, so that each block touches the yellow second inner border. Pin in place, then topstitch.

Quilting

Outline-quilt each shape in the center motif. Stitch-in-the-ditch along the outer and inner borders. Stitch-in-the-ditch diagonally and along the borders of each Pinwheel block. Stitch a large meandering design over the striped inner section. Stitch five parallel wavy lines along the outside border, breaking for the pinwheels. Bind to finish.

In Flight Sheets

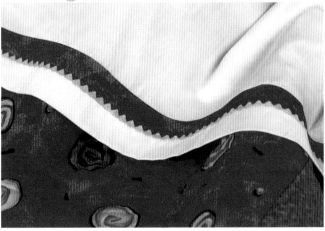

Designed and made by Jennifer Sampou.

Supplies

Bright yellow print: 1/4 yard
Red print: 1/4 yard
2 pillowcases
Twin-size top sheet

Cutting

Bright yellow print:
    Cut four 1 1/4"-wide strips; piece end to end.
Red print:
    Cut four 1 1/2"-wide strips; piece end to end.

Pillowcase Trim

1. Measure the pillowcase circumference and add 1/2". Cut 1 yellow strip and 1 red strip to this measurement.

2. Sew the ends of each strip right sides together in a 1/4" seam, to make one yellow and one red ring. Fold the yellow ring in half lengthwise, wrong side in.

3. Slip the red ring around the yellow ring, right sides together and seams and raw edges matching; pin. Slip both around the pillowcase hem, yellow side down; align the raw edges on the hem stitching, facing toward the pillowcase bottom. Pin in place. Sew the double ring to the pillowcase 1/4" from the raw edges all around.

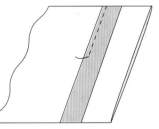

4. Flip the red strip over onto the sheet, concealing the raw edges; press. Turn the raw edge under 1/4" and topstitch.

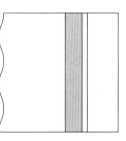

5. Using red thread, sew a decorative machine edging stitch along the exposed yellow band; position the needle so the base of the stitch falls on the seam line. Our stitch resembles a sawtooth border.

Top Sheet Trim

1. Measure the top sheet width and add 1". Cut one yellow strip and one red strip to this measurement.

2. Fold the yellow strip in half lengthwise, wrong side in. Place the red and yellow strips right sides together, raw edges matching; pin.

3. Align the raw edges, yellow side down, on the sheet's top hem stitching line, facing toward the lower hem. Pin in place, tucking in the short ends. Stitch 1/4" from the raw edges.

4. Repeat the Pillowcase Trim step 4.

5. Repeat the Pillowcase Trim step 5.

Windy Walls

Designed and painted by Jennifer Sampou using Benjamin Moore paints; see Sources.

Using chalk or a pencil, measure and mark a horizontal line on the walls all around the room about 52" from the floor. Draft and cut an arc template from posterboard. Our arc measures 38" across x 4" high. Use the arc template to mark a gently undulating line along the chalk guideline all around the room. Paint the upper wall one color, the lower wall another color. Let dry. Using a 2"-wide roller, paint a white stripe along the undulating line to separate the two color areas.

Basic Sewing Instructions

Every quilt and sewing project in this book includes a supply list, cutting instructions, and sewing instructions. Patterns are in a special section beginning on page 90. Unless otherwise specified, the yardage requirements are based on a 42" fabric width to allow for shrinkage, removal of the selvages, and variations between manufacturers. Strips are generally cut on the crosswise grain. Sometimes you will have to piece strips together end to end to obtain a longer strip. Consult a basic sewing or quiltmaking book (see page 110 for suggested titles) for help with techniques like mitering, making a continuous bias binding, making and installing piping, or tying a quilt. To make iron-on appliqués, follow the fusible web manufacturer's instructions; we recommend paper-backed fusible web because it's easier to mark. Basic instructions for making a crib bumper pad and a crib dust ruffle follow.

Basic Bumper Pad

This bumper pad is designed for a standard 27" x 52" crib mattress. Adjust the yardage and cutting measurements if your crib does not take a standard mattress.

Supplies

Fabric #1: 1 3/4 yards for the inside bumper

Fabric #2: 1 3/4 yards for the outside bumper

Batting, 10-ounce, 48"-wide: 1 5/8 yards

Ribbon: 6 1/4 yards, or 3/8 yard coordinating fabric, for ties

Piping, lace, or other trim: 4 1/2 yards (optional)

Cutting

Fabrics #1 and #2:

Cut five 12"-wide strips. Piece as necessary to cut two 28" lengths and two 53" lengths.

Batting:

Cut two 12" x 53" pieces and two 12" x 28" pieces.

Ribbon:

Cut 14 ribbon ties 16" long, or 14 fabric strips 1 1/2" x 16 1/2".

Assembly

Use a walking foot to sew this project. Sew 1/2" seams unless otherwise directed.

1. Lay the four fabric #2 pieces wrong side up. Lay batting on top. Machine-baste 3/8" from edge all around. Trim the batting as close to the stitching as possible.

2. Optional: Stabilize each section by drafting and stitching a vertical 12" line through the middle of each piece.

3. Lay out the four batted sections end to end, alternating the sizes. Stitch the sections right sides together along the 12" edges. Press the three seams open, taking care not to flatten the batting.

4. Sew the four fabric #1 pieces together end to end, and press, as in step 3.

5. Optional: Pin decorative piping or trim to one or both long raw edges of the fabric #1 piece, right sides together. Machine-baste 1/4" from edge all around.

6. Optional: To make 14 fabric ties, fold each strip in half lengthwise, right sides together. Stitch across one end and down length of strip, making 1/4" seam. Clip the corner. Turn right side out and press. Fold the remaining raw edge 1/4" to the inside and stitch closed.

7. Lay the fabric #1 bumper section right side up on a flat surface. Fold the 14 ribbon or fabric ties in half and pin folded end to the top and bottom raw edge at each seam, at each end, and at the midpoint of each larger section (on the optional stitching line made in step 2).

8. Lay the two sections right sides together; pin. Use a zipper foot to stitch a 1/2" seam all around, crowding against the piping cord (if present) for a smooth finish; leave a 9" opening in one end for turning.

Stop 1" from corner

Start 1" from corner

9. Clip corners and turn right side out. Fold in the seam allowance at the open end and topstitch closed.

An Alternate Finish:

8. Lay the two sections right sides together; pin. Stitch the bottom and side edges; leave the top edge open.

9. Clip the stitched corners, and turn right side out. Baste the top raw edges together. Bind the edge with matching or contrasting fabric.

Basic Crib Dust Ruffle

This dust ruffle skirt is designed to fit a standard 27" x 52" crib mattress and has an 18" to 22" drop. Adjust the yardage and cutting measurements if your bedding is a different size.

Supplies

Muslin: 1 1/2 yards for base

Skirt fabric: 5 1/4 yards (lengthwise cut) or 6 2/3 yards (crosswise cut); decide which cutting option below works best for your fabric.

Cutting

Muslin:

Cut one 27" x 52" rectangle.

Skirt fabric:

Cut in half lengthwise, then cut a 62 1/2" length and a 125" length from each piece.

Or:

Cut fabric crosswise into ten 24"-wide strips. Piece as necessary to cut two 62 1/2" lengths and two 125" lengths.

Assembly

1. On each panel, narrow-hem the short edges and make a 1" hem on one long edge. You can omit the 1" hems if all four panels have an attractive selvage.

2. Gather the top raw edge of each panel by zigzagging over a string or cord laid along the 1/2" seamline; take care not to catch the string in the stitching.

3. Pull the string of a shorter panel and draw the gathers as closely as possible. Release the string. Open up and adjust the gathered edge to fit a shorter edge of the muslin base less 1". Pin, right sides together. Machine-stitch 1/2" from the edge on the gathering line. Repeat to gather and join each skirt panel to the muslin base.

4. Overcast or serge the seam to finish.

Tree Sketch

Bunny
Cut 10

"B"

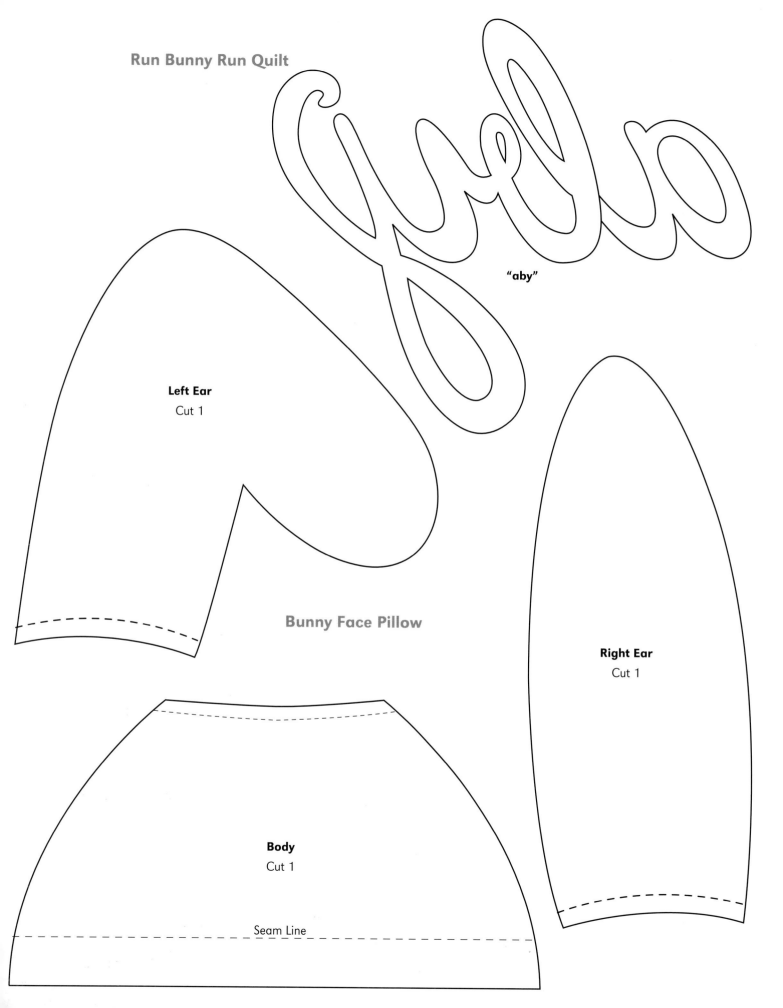

"aby"

Left Ear
Cut 1

Bunny Face Pillow

Right Ear
Cut 1

Body
Cut 1

Seam Line

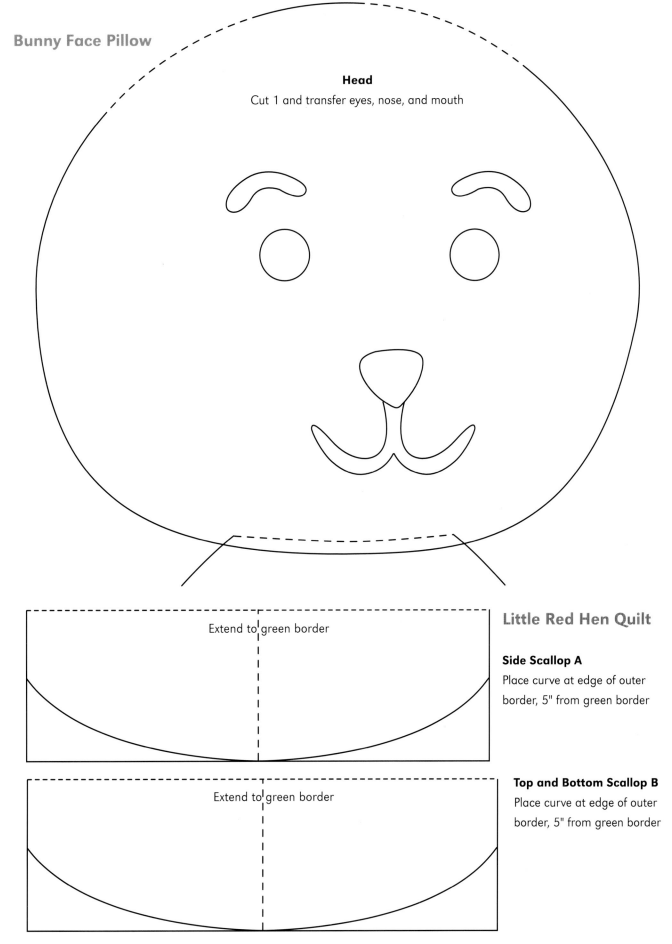

Bunny Face Pillow

Head
Cut 1 and transfer eyes, nose, and mouth

Extend to green border

Extend to green border

Little Red Hen Quilt

Side Scallop A
Place curve at edge of outer border, 5" from green border

Top and Bottom Scallop B
Place curve at edge of outer border, 5" from green border

Little Red Hen Quilt

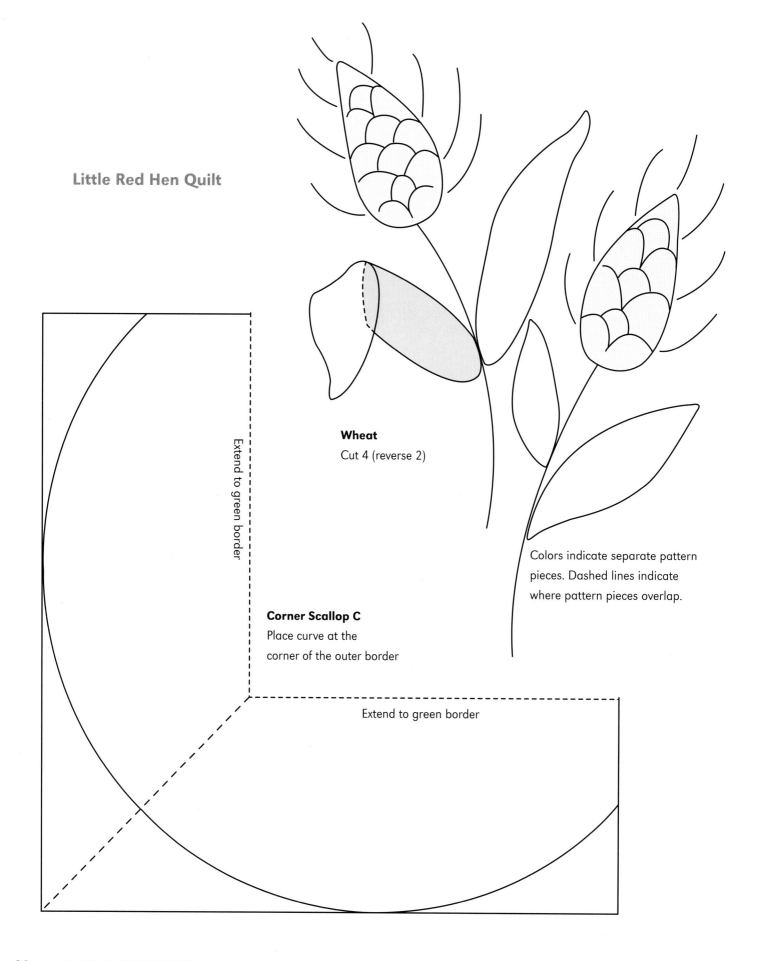

Wheat
Cut 4 (reverse 2)

Colors indicate separate pattern pieces. Dashed lines indicate where pattern pieces overlap.

Extend to green border

Corner Scallop C
Place curve at the
corner of the outer border

Extend to green border

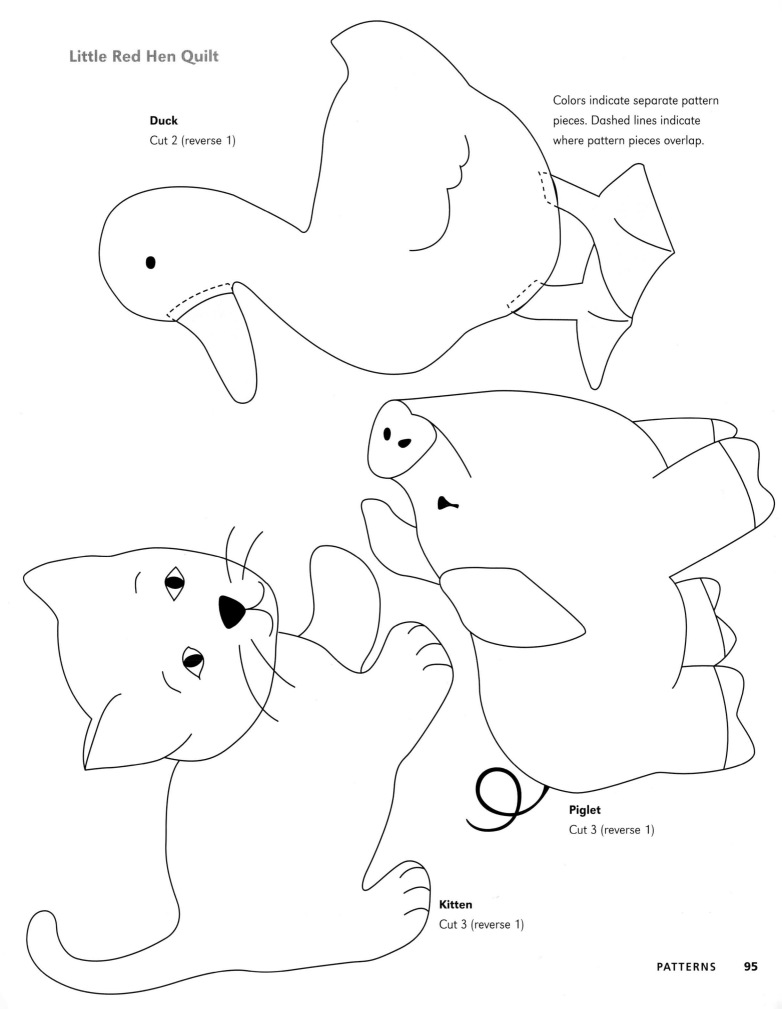

Little Red Hen Quilt

Duck
Cut 2 (reverse 1)

Colors indicate separate pattern pieces. Dashed lines indicate where pattern pieces overlap.

Piglet
Cut 3 (reverse 1)

Kitten
Cut 3 (reverse 1)

Colors indicate separate pattern
pieces. Dashed lines indicate
where pattern pieces overlap.

Cut 1

Little Red Hen Quilt

Cut 1

Little Red Hen Quilt

Cut 1

Colors indicate separate pattern
pieces. Dashed lines indicate
where pattern pieces overlap.

Cut 1

"Who will plant this wheat?" asked the Little Red Hen.

"Not I," said the pig, duck and cat.

So the Little Red Hen did it herself

"Who will eat the bread?"

"We will!" the lazy ones cried.

"No," said the Hen. "I shall eat it."

Little Red Hen Quilt   Enlarge 225% and center on yellow-and-white check fabric.

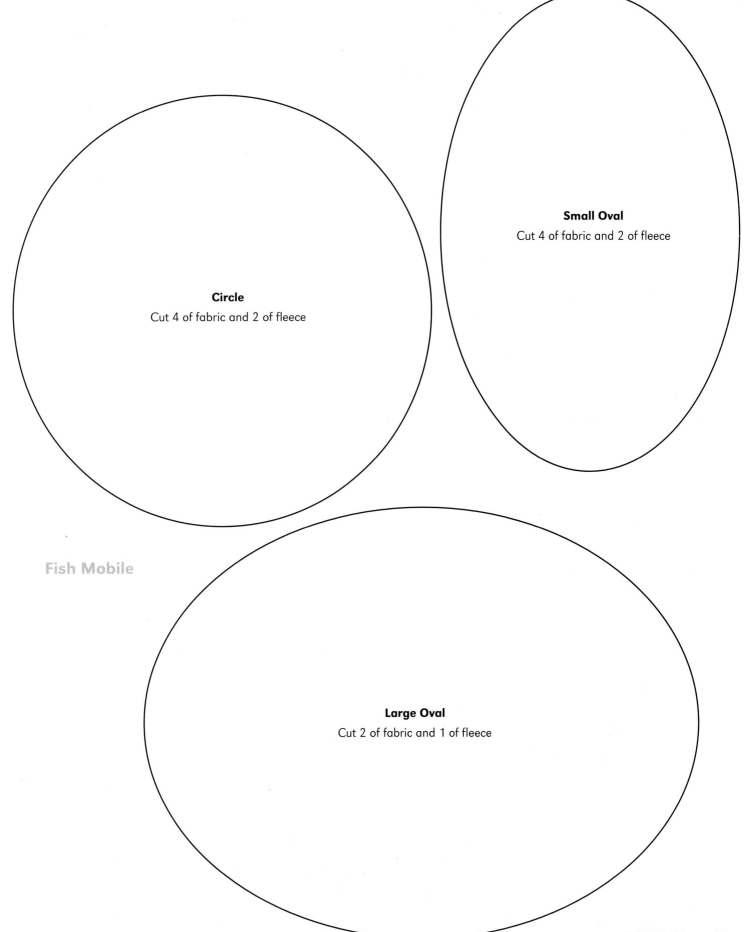

Circle

Cut 4 of fabric and 2 of fleece

Small Oval

Cut 4 of fabric and 2 of fleece

Fish Mobile

Large Oval

Cut 2 of fabric and 1 of fleece

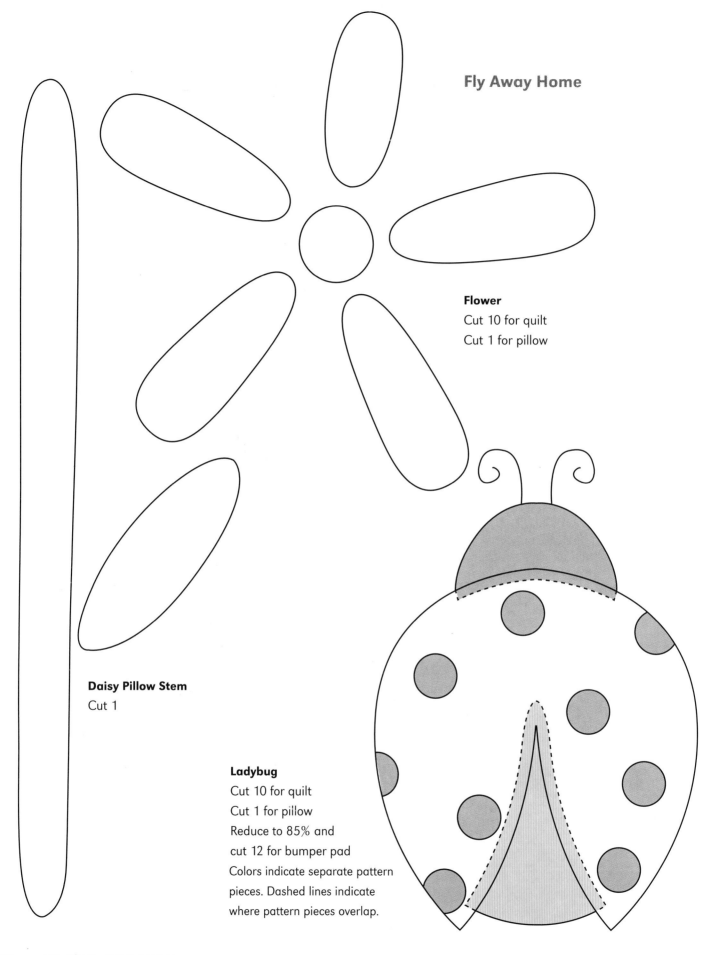

Fly Away Home

Flower
Cut 10 for quilt
Cut 1 for pillow

Daisy Pillow Stem
Cut 1

Ladybug
Cut 10 for quilt
Cut 1 for pillow
Reduce to 85% and
cut 12 for bumper pad
Colors indicate separate pattern
pieces. Dashed lines indicate
where pattern pieces overlap.

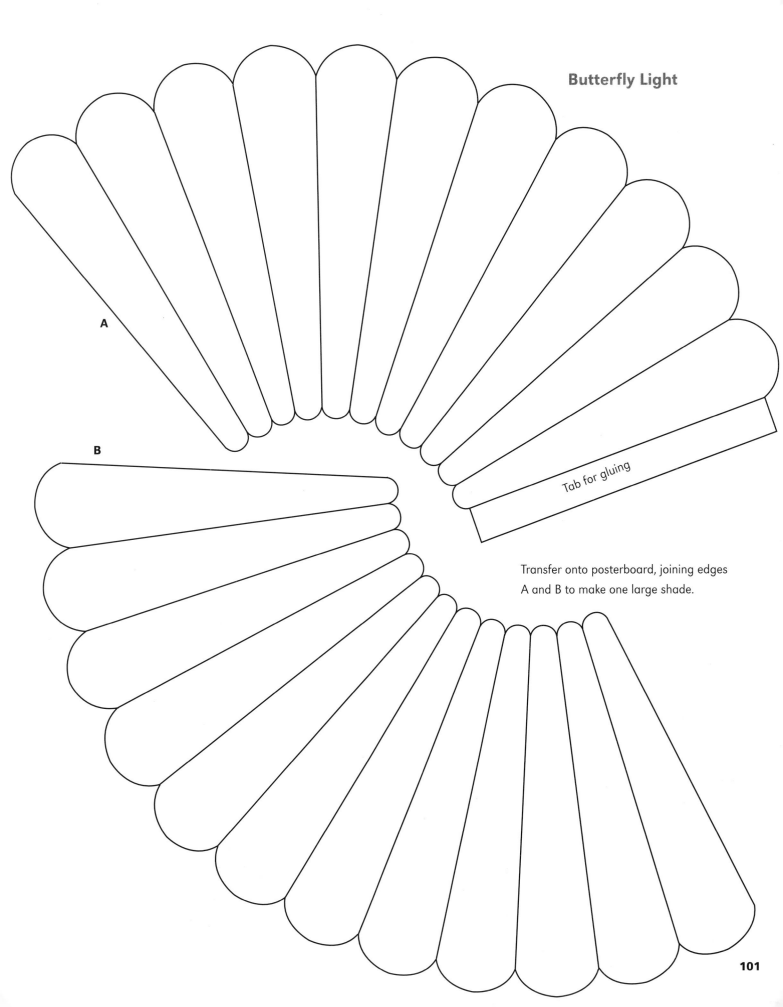

Butterfly Light

A

B

Tab for gluing

Transfer onto posterboard, joining edges
A and B to make one large shade.

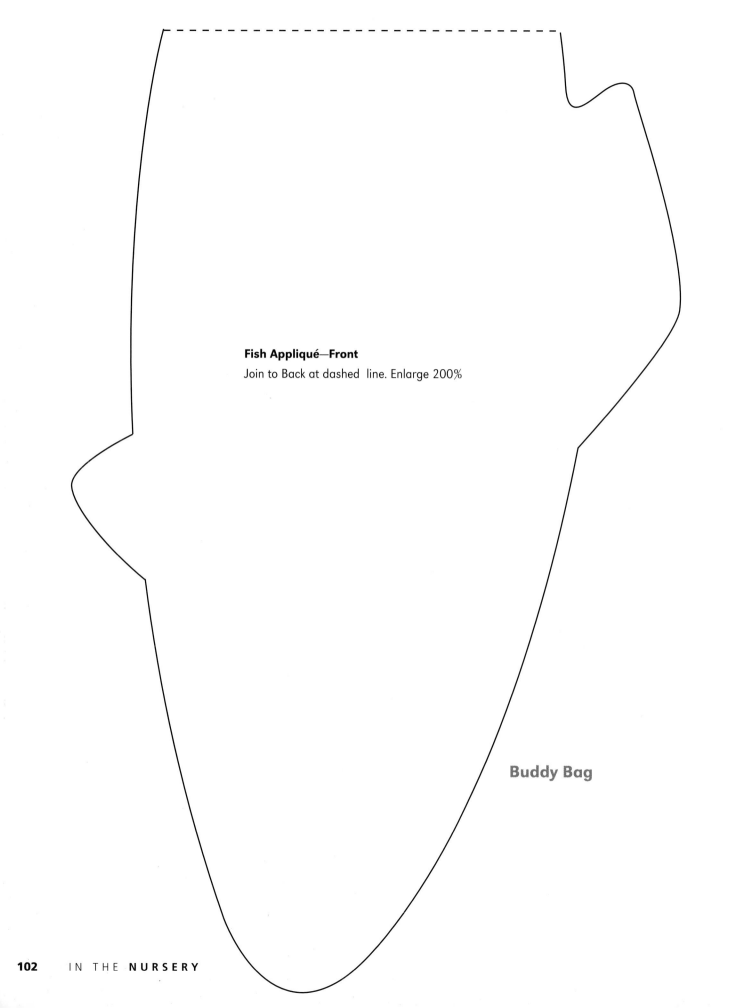

Fish Appliqué—Front

Join to Back at dashed line. Enlarge 200%

Buddy Bag

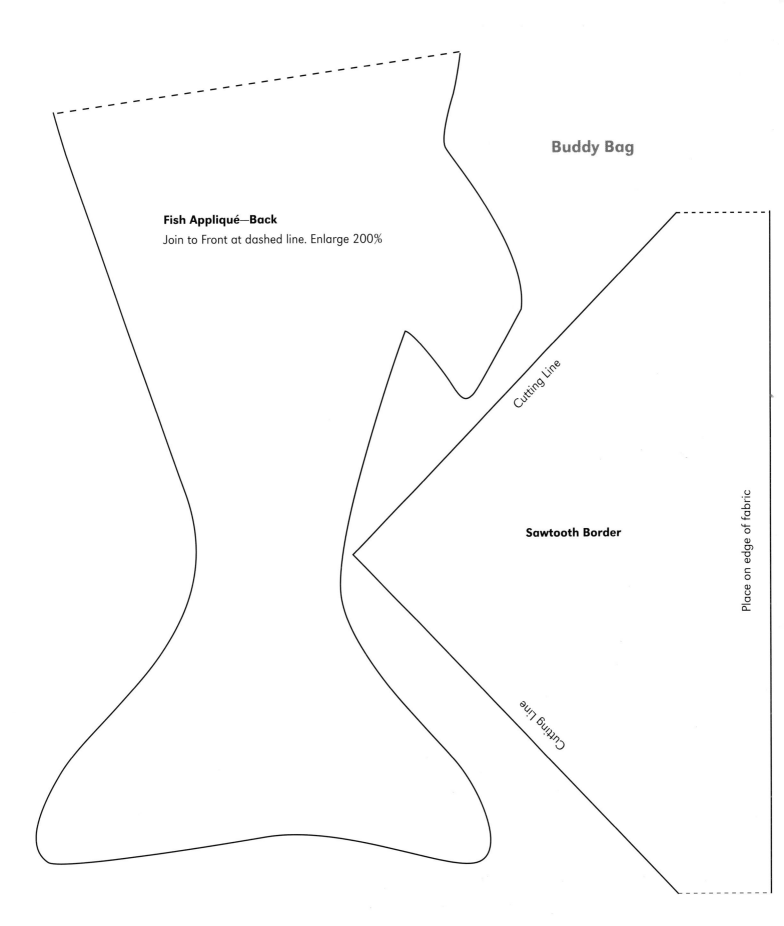

Buddy Bag

Fish Appliqué—Back

Join to Front at dashed line. Enlarge 200%

Cutting Line

Sawtooth Border

Place on edge of fabric

Cutting Line

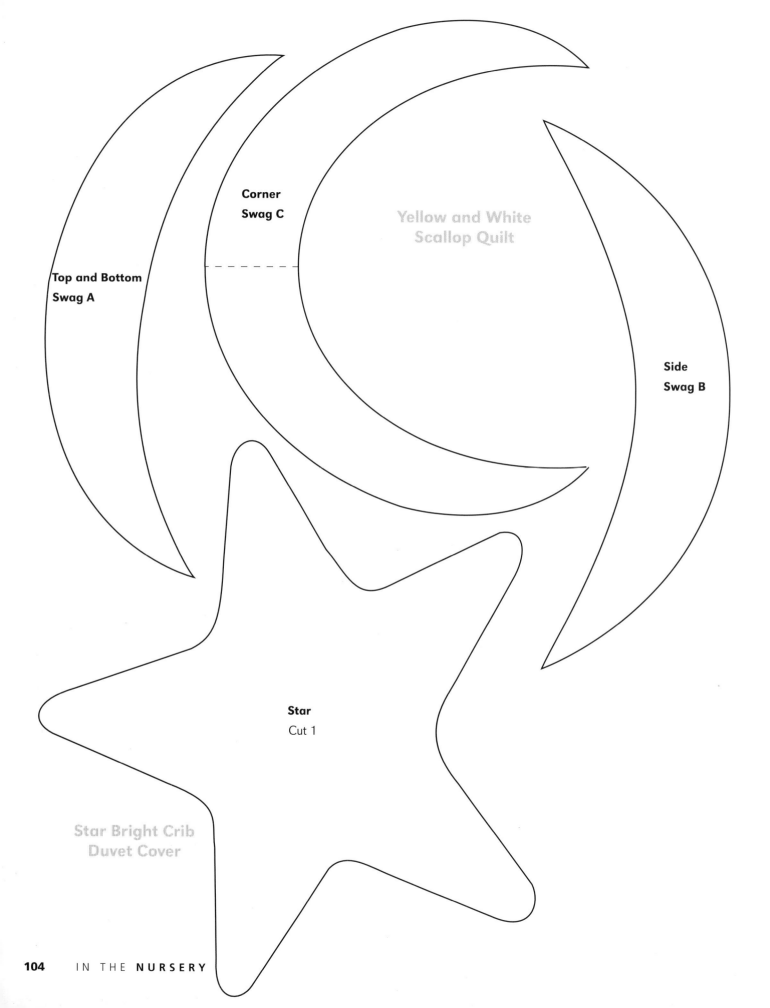

Corner
Swag C

Yellow and White
Scallop Quilt

Top and Bottom
Swag A

Side
Swag B

Star
Cut 1

Star Bright Crib
Duvet Cover

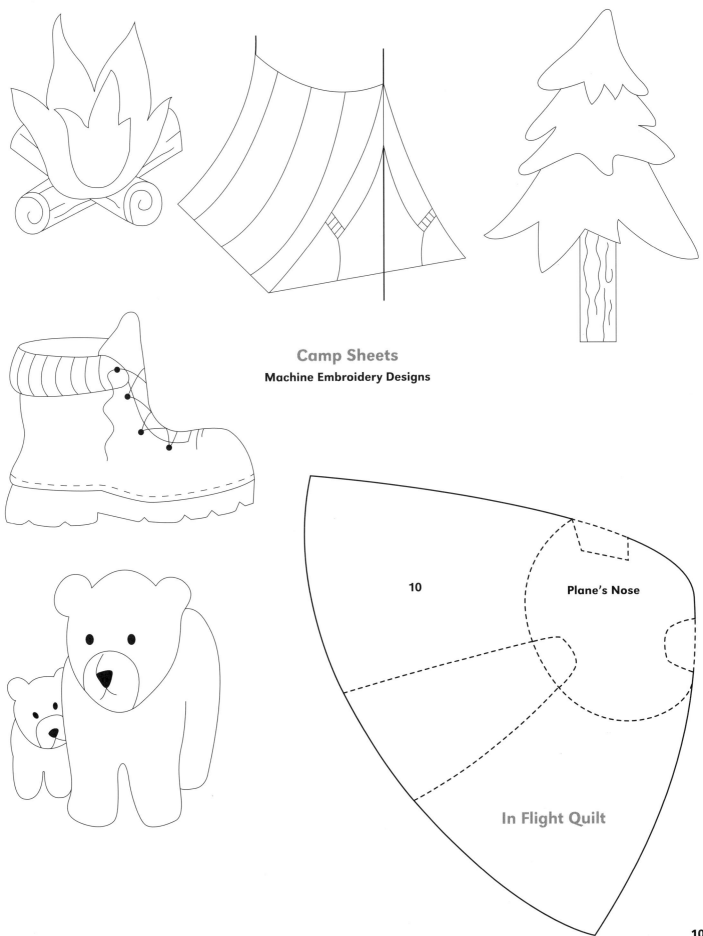

Camp Sheets

Machine Embroidery Designs

10

Plane's Nose

In Flight Quilt

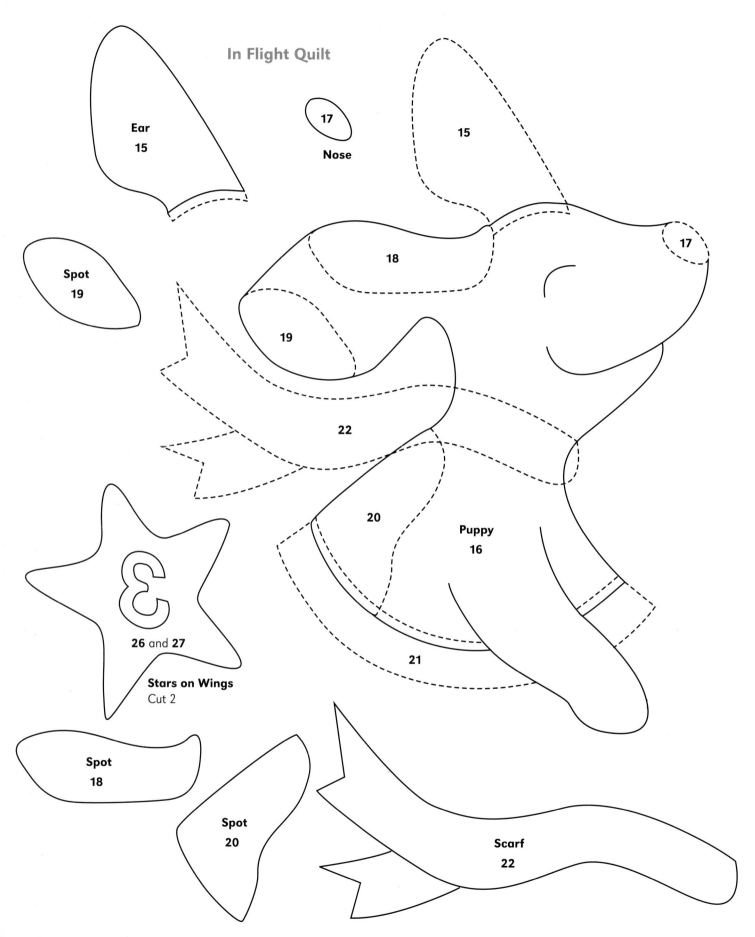

In Flight Quilt

Ear
15

17
Nose

15

Spot
19

18

17

19

22

20

Puppy
16

26 and 27
Stars on Wings
Cut 2

21

Spot
18

Spot
20

Scarf
22

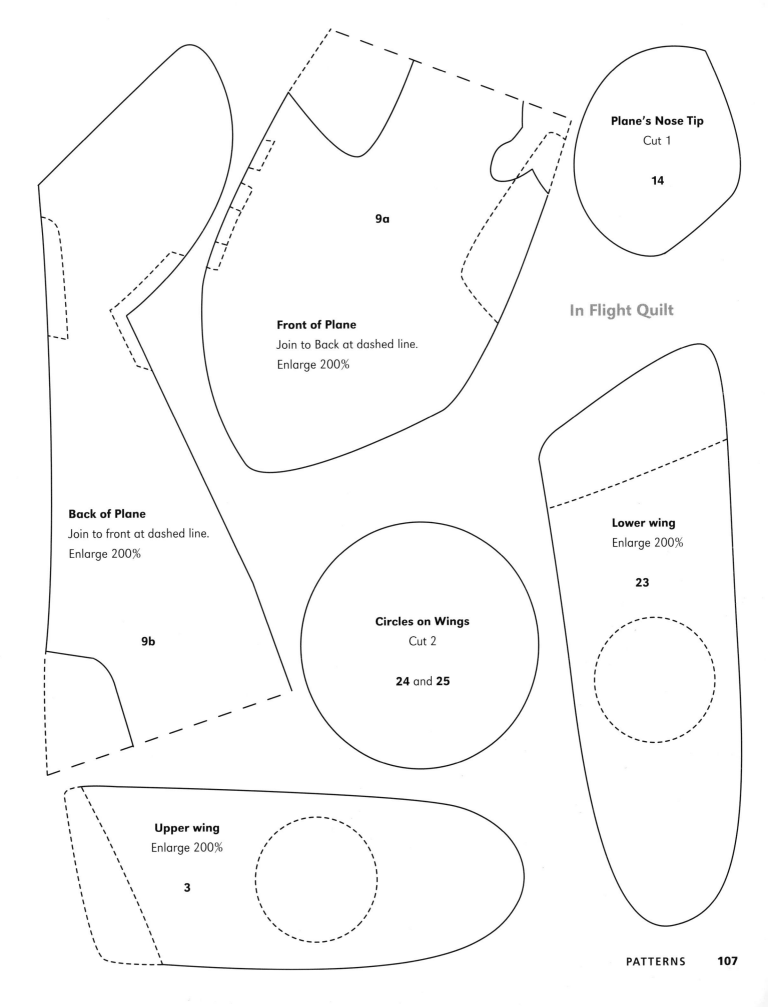

Plane's Nose Tip
Cut 1

14

9a

Front of Plane
Join to Back at dashed line.
Enlarge 200%

In Flight Quilt

Back of Plane
Join to front at dashed line.
Enlarge 200%

9b

Lower wing
Enlarge 200%

23

Circles on Wings
Cut 2

24 and **25**

Upper wing
Enlarge 200%

3

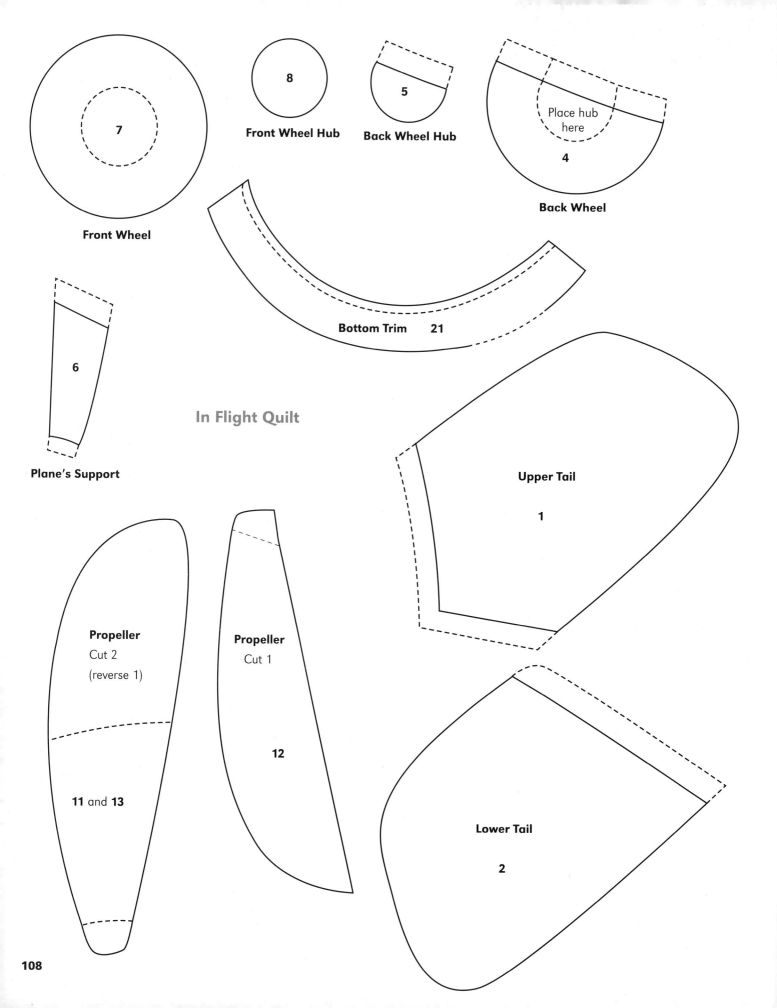

Front Wheel

7

8
Front Wheel Hub

5
Back Wheel Hub

4
Place hub here
Back Wheel

Bottom Trim   21

6
Plane's Support

In Flight Quilt

Upper Tail
1

Propeller
Cut 2
(reverse 1)

11 and 13

Propeller
Cut 1

12

Lower Tail
2

Sources

FINDING IT

Room 1: A Sweet Lullaby

Cream chenille cradle set, Bellissimo crib blanket, antique doorknob rack, Claudette ottoman, patchwork stroller blanket from *Lou Lou's*, Tiverton, RI, 401-624-8231, www.loulousdecor.com (under construction). Antique reproduction dolls and "treasures" from *Susan Haltzman Collections*, Barrington, RI, 401-245-3277. Floorcloth canvas from *Gregory D. Dorrance Co.*, Attleboro, MA, 508-222-6255. Antique White Aquavelvet wall paint, Platinum Gray Porch and Floor Enamel from *Benjamin Moore*, 800-672-4686, www.benjaminmoore.com. Photographed at the home of Carolyn and Peter Schmitz, Newport, RI.

Room 2: Run Bunny Run

Quilt features Scallop, Star, and Scroll fabrics from the Jennifer Sampou Designer Essentials collection and Dot from the Jennifer Sampou Rainforest collection; bumper pad features Star and Dot; lampshade slipcover features Scroll; see buying information below right. Judi Boisson hand-knitted rug, feather star cornflower quilt from *Lou Lou's*, Tiverton, RI, 401-624-8231, www.loulousdecor.com (under construction). Custom lampshade slipcover from *Gloria MacKenzie*, Barrington, RI, 401-245-0235. Wastebasket from *Wendy Neale Decoupage*, Middletown, RI, 401-849-3431. Chenille craft cuts and yardage from *Daisy Kingdom*, a division of Springs Industries; call 800-333-5820 for retailer near you; wwwdaisykingdom.com. Aquavelvet 820 wall paint, Flat 820 paint (half-recipe) on ceiling from *Benjamin Moore*, 800-672-4686, www.benjaminmoore.com. Photographed at the home of Carolyn and Peter Schmitz, Newport, RI.

Room 3: Little Red Hen

Pier house rugs from *Lou Lou's*, Tiverton, RI, 401-624-8231, www.loulousdecor.com (under construction). Kona Snow quilt backing fabric by *Robert Kaufman Fine Fabrics*; call 800-877-2066 for retailer near you or check your local quilting, fabric, or craft store. Linen White Aquavelvet wall paint topped with a colorwash glaze mixed with Beacon Hill Damask HC2, both from *Benjamin Moore*, 800-672-4686, www.benjaminmoore.com. Photographed at the home of Andre and Elsa Sampou, West Barnstable, MA.

Room 4: Star Bright

Fish mobile features Fish and Water fabrics from the Jennifer Sampou Red Sea collection; see buying information at right. Sofa and rugs from *Bellini Juvenile Design Furniture*; call 1 888-77BABY1 for location nearest you. Sun Ray quilt

from *Simply Stars* by Alex Anderson, C&T Publishing, Concord, CA, 800-284-1114, www.ctpub.com. Crib bumper pad, sheet, and dust ruffle from *Cotton Tail Designs*; call 800-628-2621 or e-mail info@cottontaledesigns.com for retailer near you. Window sheers and down comforter from *Pottery Barn Kids*, 800-430-7373. Drawer pulls from *Land of Nod*, 800-933-9904, www.landofnod.com. Provence Crème 2021-60 Aquavelvet wall paint, Costa Rica Blue 2064-50 Aquavelvet topped with white glaze on ceiling and upper border, Sweet Orange 2017-40 and Tangelo 2017-30 Aquavelvet on lower border; all paints from *Benjamin Moore*, 800-672-4686, www.benjaminmoore.com. Photographed at the home of Jennifer Sampou and Todd Hensley, Lafayette, CA.

Room 5: Camping Out

Quilt features Star and Hatching fabrics from the Jennifer Sampou Designer Essentials collection, Leaf from the Jennifer Sampou Rainforest collection, Sky and Petroglyphs from the Jennifer Sampou Native Plains collection; see buying information below right. Assorted plaids and stripes from *Robert Kaufman Fine Fabrics*; call 800-877-2066 for retailer near you or check your local quilting, fabric, or craft store. Bear rug and dog pillow from *Chandler Four Corners*, Manchester Center, VT, 800-239-5137, chandlr4@sover.net. Canvas supplies from *Gregory D. Dorrance Co.*, Attleboro, MA, 508-222-6255. All other furnishings from *Goodnight Room*, Oakland, CA, 510-601-6390. Isacord embroidery thread, stabilizer from *Oklahoma Embroidery and Supply*, www.Embroideryonline.com, or through your local Bernina dealer, 888-237-6462, www.berninausa.com. Photographed at *Goodnight Room*, Oakland, CA.

Room 6: Fly Away Home

Quilt and ladybug pillow feature Scroll, Scallop Dot, and Hatching fabrics from the Jennifer Sampou Designer Essentials collection, Dot from the Jennifer Sampou Rainforest collection, and Daisy and Leaf from the Jennifer Sampou Flower Market collection; see buying information at right. Picket fence headboard painted with 1653 Semi-gloss, floor with 1653 Floor Enamel topped with a glaze mixed from 1654; all paints from *Pratt & Lambert*, 800-BUY-PRATT, www.prattandlambert.com. Butterfly light from *Wendy Neale Decoupage*, Middletown, RI, 401-849-3431. Welcome Light and chandelier clips from *The Candle Station*, Ashville, NC, 800-552-4003, www.candlestation.com, cstation@brinet.com. Children's clothing, daisy purse, pull toy from *Michael Hayes for Kids*, Newport, RI, 401-846-8390, mhayes2389@aol.com. Photographed at the home of Carolyn and Peter Schmitz, Newport, RI.

Room 7: Yellow Ribbons

Quilt features assorted yellow fabrics from the Jennifer Sampou Designer Essentials, Paisley, Red Sea, and Flower Market collections; buying information below. Kona Snow quilt center panel and border fabric from *Robert Kaufman Fine Fabrics*; call 800-877-2066 for retailer near you or check your local quilting, fabric, or craft store. Sheets, pillow, fleece blanket from *The Linen Shop*, Newport RI, 401-846-0225. Hooked rug from *Pottery Barn*, 800-430-7373. Bowling Bunnies from *Kelly+Gillis*, Newport, RI, 401-849-7380. Suntan Yellow Aquavelvet wall paint topped with Linen White glaze and White Satin Impervo trim paint from *Benjamin Moore*, 800-672-4686, www.benjaminmoore.com. Photographed at the home of Anne and Chris Glazzard, Barrington, RI.

Room 8: In Flight

Quilt features Swirl, Textures, and Dots fabrics from the Jennifer Sampou Calypso collection, Star, Leaf, and Dot from the Jennifer Sampou Rainforest collection, Scroll, Go Mice Go, and Sky from the Jennifer Sampou Designer Essentials collection, and Circle from the Jennifer Sampou Red Sea collection; see buying information below. Beanbag, U.S.A. vintage map, green basket, plane clock, frame from *Goodnight Room*, Oakland, CA, 510-601-6390. Window treatment and dust ruffle from *Furbelows Fabrics*, Alamo, CA, 925-837-8579. Airplane lamp from *Target*, www.target.com. Airplane pegs from *Land of Nod*, 800-933-9904, www.landofnod.com. Chenille craft cuts and yardage from *Daisy Kingdom*, a division of Springs Industries; call 800-333-5820 for retailer near you; wwwdaisykingdom.com. Cottontail 2155-70 upper wall paint, White Satin 2067-70 lower wall paint, Decorators White trim paint, and Vermillion 2002-01 bookcase and hutch trim paint from *Benjamin Moore*, 800-672-4686, www.benjaminmoore.com. Photographed at the home of Michele and Jon Henderson, Lafayette, CA.

Jennifer Sampou Fabrics

Ask for Jennifer Sampou fabrics, including the new In the Nursery collection designed by Jennifer and her sister Carolyn Schmitz, at your local quilting or fabric store. For mail-order availability, contact:

Cotton Patch Mail Order
3405 Hall Lane, Dept. CTB
Lafayette, CA 94549
800-835-4418 or 925-283-7883
quiltusa@yahoo.com, www.quiltusa.com

Wholesale information: Robert Kaufman Fine Fabrics, 800-877-2066, www.robertkaufman.com.

Paint sources:

Benjamin Moore Co., www.benjaminmoore.com; call 800-672-4686 for retailer near you.

Pratt and Lambert., www.prattandlambert.com; call 800-BUY-PRATT for retailer near you.

MAKING IT

Books

Drucker, Mindy and Pierre Finkelstein. *Recipes for Surfaces: Decorative Paint Finishes Made Simple*. New York: Fireside/Simon & Schuster Inc., 1993. This book is great for beginners. It gives very easy-to-follow instructions on glazing techniques and very helpful information on color and how to use it.

Hargrave, Harriet. *Mastering Machine Appliqué: The Satin Stitch, Mock Hand Appliqué and Other Techniques*. Lafayette, CA: C&T Publishing, Inc., 1992. The complete guide to machine appliqué covering the satin stitch and mock hand appliqué. Includes specific equipment, supplies, preparation methods, and techniques for each type of stitching.

Hargrave, Harriet and Sharyn Craig. *The Art of Classic Quiltmaking*. Lafayette, CA: C&T Publishing, Inc., 2000. A complete reference guide and ultimate how-to book for quiltmakers.

Innes, Jocasta. *The New Paint Magic*. New York: Pantheon Books, 1992. This updated version is one of the author's best decorative painting handbooks, covering many finishes from ragging to rubber-stamping. It has great ideas and photographs but is best suited for those who have some experience with painting. It covers walls, floors, floorcloths, furniture, and fundamentals. Other books by the same author that are worth looking at include: *Paint Magic*. New York: Pantheon Books, 1981. *Decorating with Paint*. New York: Harmony Books, 1986.

Montano, Judith. *The Crazy Quilt Handbook*. Lafayette, CA: C&T Publishing, Inc., 1986. An excellent reference guide and how-to for crazy quilting.

Leaflets

Quilting Basics. Little Rock, AR: Leisure Arts, Inc., 1999. A concise, informative reference guide for adding both squared and mitered borders, making a continuous bias strip for binding or piping, making straight-grain binding, attaching binding with mitered corners, and attaching binding with overlapped corners.

Pillow Making. Little Rock, AR: Leisure Arts, Inc., 1999. This guide shows several styles of pillows to make and includes instructions on adding cording (piping).

Wonderful Walls with Paint. Little Rock, AR: Leisure Arts Inc., 1999. This reference covers basic tools, special products, surface preparation, and painting guidelines. Techniques include glazing, cross-hatching, striping, combing, rag rolling, sponging, stenciling, and colorwashing.

Faux Finishes. Little Rock, AR: Leisure Arts Inc., 1999. Techniques for transforming furniture and decorative accessories. Includes instructions for the following finishes: malachite, marbling, crackle, tortoiseshell, plastic wrapping, combing, wood graining, distressed, rusting, and verdigris.

Decorative Painting. Little Rock, AR: Leisure Arts Inc., 1999. An informative guide to the brush types and basic strokes needed to paint fruit, flowers, and leaves.

Video

Montano, Judith Baker. *Crazy Quilting*. Lafayette, CA: C&T Publishing, Inc., 1996. Running Time: 60 minutes. A companion to *The Crazy Quilt Handbook*. Techniques, tips, and design applications inspire you to create your own crazy quilt masterpiece.

Web Sites

www.quiltvillage.com
This web site is by *Better Homes & Gardens*. It gives some basic quiltmaking instructions.

www.crazyquilters.com
Read instructions for making continuous bias and stitching a crazy quilt. The site also includes tips and a chart of standard quilt sizes.

www.paintquality.com
Special area for do-it-yourselfers. Best paint web site. Has steps to success for interior painting, encyclopedia of paint terms, FAQ's (frequently asked questions), Problem Solver. Paint suppliers and links to other good web sites. Easy to follow and very well organized.

www.fauxlikeapro.com
Tricks of the trade for decorative painting. Online store for starter kits, glazes, paints, tools, how-to books and videos. Q and A section is also good.

PLAYING IT SAFE

Safety is a great concern for all parents. Most accidents can be avoided with planning, preparation, and diligent baby watching, especially from birth to two years of age. Today's books, internet sites, and consumer organizations make it easy for parents to stay informed. Below are some topics of particular concern, followed by sources you can consult for more information.

Sleeping

All new cribs sold in the United States today must meet the Consumer Product Safety Commission (CPSC) standards. If you are using an older crib, check for the following features to ensure the safety of your child:

- Crib slats no more than 2 3/8" apart so baby cannot slip his or her head or torso through.
- Mattress fits tight, with no more than two fingers' width between the mattress and crib to prevent baby from getting caught. A standard crib mattress is 27 1/2" x 51 7/8".
- Drop sides that lower only partway and have a double-action latch to prevent accidental lowering.
- If the crib is vintage or secondhand, be sure the paint is not cracking, loose, or lead-based, and that the construction is sturdy.

The CPSC recommends that "a baby under 12 months of age be put to sleep in a crib on his back with no soft bedding." Much of the concern regarding soft bedding is possible suffocation and Sudden Infant Death Syndrome (SIDS). The CPSC also recommends removing "pillows, quilts, comforters, sheepskins, stuffed toys, and other soft products" from the crib and to consider dressing baby in a sleeper and omitting a blanket or other covering. The crib mattress should be firm. The sheet should be tight-fitting with good-quality elastic all around, not just at the corners. Bumpers should have at least 12 ties on top and bottom. Avoid putting baby on waterbeds, beanbags, or an adult bed that faces a wall, as baby could fall into the crack.

Accessories

Keep all framed artwork and shelving out of baby's reach. Tie dangling window cords up out of baby's reach. Push furniture in front of electrical outlets and install outlet covers on any without furniture blocking them. Other potential hazards include heaters, unsturdy furniture, and floor lamps.

Pregnant Woman Warning

While today's latex paints are safer to use than previous generations of paint, it's still wise for pregnant women to leave the painting to someone else. Good ventilation is essential both during and after the job. Ideally, fumes should be allowed to dissipate before the expecting mom returns home. The same goes for installing new carpets with backings that could give off harmful toxins to mom or baby.

For Further Information

The CPSC offers free brochures highlighting low-cost ways to childproof your home. For information, contact:
CPSC
Att: Publications
4330 East-West Highway
Bethesda, MD 20814-4408
www.cpsc.gov

www.about.com
Go to the parenting/family heading. This is a great beginning point to research baby info on the web. About.com's network of sites includes over 700 highly targeted environments, each overseen by a professional guide.

www.babydata.com
This pregnancy site is full of interesting and current information for expecting moms.

www.babycenter.com
This site has everything parents need to know about their baby, including a special area devoted to safety issues from infant to toddlerhood, great links, recommended reading list, and online shopping. It's also easy to navigate.

www.cpsc.gov
The US Consumer Product Safety Commission provides the most up-to-date recall list of manufactured items and information regarding all safety issues for products.

www.Parentsplace.com
This site offers a comprehensive list of child safety topics, including first aid, baby care, and recall notices. The information is thorough and concise.

Index

About the authors

Jennifer Sampou

Jennifer Sampou is a leading textile designer in the quilting industry. Since 1989 she has designed and styled over two thousand fabrics that have sold over eight million yards. Jennifer has traveled the world gathering inspiration for her designs and is known for her diverse hand and exceptional color sense. She has been featured in major quilt magazines, and she lectures to fabric enthusiasts everywhere.

Jennifer has a degree in Surface Design from the Fashion Institute of Technology in New York and a Bachelor of Science degree in Textiles from the University of Vermont. After serving as Creative Director for P&B Textiles for seven years, she decided, at age 30, that she was ready to start a family. In order to continue her career, she opened her own home-based business, Studio Sampou, in Lafayette, California. Currently she licenses her designs to Robert Kaufman Company in Los Angeles. Most importantly, she enjoys relaxing with her loving husband Todd, being home to raise their son Thomas, and spending time in nature with her black labrador Sunny .

Carolyn Sampou Schmitz

Carolyn Sampou Schmitz is one of the most gifted and talented decorative painters working today in the southeastern Massachusetts and Rhode Island area. Her designs have been featured in such books and magazines as *Victoria*, *Bon Appetit*, *Rhode Island Monthly*, *Cape Cod Life*, *Newport Life*, *The Bathroom Idea Book*, and *The Providence Journal Magazine*. She has been selected to participate in prestigous designer show houses throughout New England, and her own homes have been sought after for tours and been granted awards for historic preservation and paint colors. Carolyn has also designed children's furniture, and she recently collaborated on a line of children's fabric with her sister Jennifer.

Carolyn holds a Bachelor of Fine Arts degree from the University of Massachusetts—Amherst and Sir John Cass School of Art in London, and she continues to study art at the Rhode Island School of Design (RISD) in Providence, Rhode Island. She left a successful career in graphic design in 1990 to pursue her passion for decorative arts. Carolyn resides in Newport, Rhode Island, with her husband Peter, two children Chlöe and Dylan, and favorite companion Daisy.

Other Fine Books from C&T Publishing

Free Stuff for Collectors on the Internet, Judy Heim and Gloria Hansen
Free Stuff for Crafty Kids on the Internet, Judy Heim and Gloria Hansen
Free Stuff for Home Décor on the Internet, Judy Heim and Gloria Hansen
Free Stuff for Quilters on the Internet, 2nd Ed., Judy Heim and Gloria Hansen
Pieced Roman Shades: Turn Your Favorite Quilt Patterns into Window Hangings, Terrell Sundermann
Quilt It for Kids: 11 Projects, Sports, Fantasy & Animal Themes, Quilts for Children of All Ages, Pam Bono

Quilting with the Muppets, The Jim Henson Company in Association with Sesame Workshop
Simply Stars: Quilts that Sparkle, Alex Anderson
Special Delivery Quilts, Patrick Lose

For more information write for a free catalog:
C&T Publishing, Inc.
P.O. Box 1456
Lafayette, CA 94549
800-284-1114
http://www.ctpub.com
e-mail: ctinfo@ctpub.com